I0187847

SILENTLY BETRAYED

VOL. 1

Latosha Faulkner

Copyright © July 2020 by Latosha Faulkner. All rights reserved. No portion of this publication may be reproduced, transmitted in any forms, distributed by any means, including recording, photocopying or screenshotting, scanning by electric or mechanical methods in any manner whatsoever, without the express written permission of the publisher. The only exception is that of which is permitted under the copyrighting law such as brief quotations, including noncommercial uses with the insertion of credit citations and so forth.

For permission to use manuscript, please contact the author. To order in bulks and receive a discount, you may contact the Distributing Company, IngramSpark.

Book Development Credit goes to: Latosha Faulkner (Author), Tayla Viego (Author Photo), Aurora Publishing (Editor), and Word-2-Kindle (Cover Design & Copyediting).

Library of Congress Control Number (LCCN): 2020912324

Silently Betrayed, Series Vol.1   Paperback ISBN 978-1-7350076-0-1
E-Book ISBN 978-17350076-2-5   Hardback ISBN 978-17350076-1-8

Publisher: DefeatdaPurpose, LLC
Author: Latosha Faulkner
Attention: Copyrighting Permission
Email: defeatdapurpose@gmail.com

Distributing Company: IngramSpark
Telephone: 1 (855)-997-7275
Email: ingramsparkinfo@ingramcontent.com
& customerservice@ingramcontent.com

Orders by U.S. trade bookstores and wholesalers.
Please contact Ingram Publisher Services, Tel: 1 (800) 937-8200 or
1 (800)-937-8000
Email: orders@ingrambook.com

International Orders
Telephone:1 (615)-793-5000 ext.27652
Email: ii.orders@ingrambook.com

Christian/Spring Arbor
Telephone: 1 (800)-395-4340
Email: customerservice@springarbor.com

First Printed in the United States of America

Fictional Book
Warning

DEFEAT DA Purpose LLC
defeatdapurpose@gmail.com

This book is fictional and inspired by true events. At no point can you, as the reader, pinpoint true characters.

Acknowledgments

ONLY A FEW OF MY SUPPORTERS knew I was writing this book to enlighten people who are living with HIV, while helping others remain HIV negative. As we all should know, HIV has no age, no name, no location, and anyone who is having unprotected sex is at risk. This book is inspired by real life situations that's going unnoticed around the world.

My main goal is to bring light to those living with HIV, without judgement, while educating others in the hopes of decreasing stigma. I appreciate all the words of encouragement in proceeding with my goals. A special thanks to my best friend, mother, family, and friends for being the biggest supporters of my book, along with my overall life. I would like to thank some of my readers in the Upcoming Authors group for giving me advice and pushing me along the way. I never thought this day would come, but it's here. We all are facing different challenges in life and one challenge shouldn't outweigh another. I say that to say this, *"Just because the bullet didn't hit you, doesn't mean you forget how close you were to that bullet."* I pray that you read this book with an unbiased mind, and I look forward to replying directly to my readers as they voice their opinions.

TABLE OF CONTENTS

Section 1

Prologue...ix

Chapter 1: Childhood Flashbacks...................................1

Chapter 2: Falling In and Out of Love 9

Chapter 3: Two Doors Open...27

Chapter 4: Who Do I Choose?..36

Chapter 5: Routine Check Up & Results 43

Chapter 6: Victim All Over Again..................................58

Chapter 7: Am I Living or Dying?..................................67

Chapter 8: Can I Still Live? 80

Section 2: Postscript

Quotes by the Author..93

TIPS - Don't Become a Victim to HIV 95

Q&A by the Author...99

Message from the Author 103

Contact the Author 105

Bibliography..107

PROLOGUE

I BECAME A CREATURE OF my own regrets and built-up sins. Spending many of my nights tossing and turning, restless. It was 3:00 am, but I found myself looking at the wall, my brows furrowed in confusion. As I sat there staring, I noticed in my peripheral, a mirror. I turned my head, looking at the reflection of myself. Ashamed! I was very ashamed of me! I realized that I was inside a body I no longer wanted to be attached to. So much was wrong, and I needed a way out. I had no solution to my problems because the puzzle facing me was just too hard to solve. I was fighting a battle in silence that I could no longer fight alone.

I was drifting away. My life was indescribably distorted. Standing at a dead end, facing the truth was all I had left to do. After taking so many deep breaths, I asked myself, "What in the world is wrong with me?" Something was wrong inside of me and every day that became clearer and clearer.

Fear covered my mind as I imagined being disowned. "I just didn't care anymore! Tell me why…why I should feel like a prisoner in my own skin?" I was ready to…I was ready to reveal the truth at all costs. All these feelings came rushing down on me as I began to lay back in bed to rest for later that day. I was indeed ready to tell my family, friends, teachers, and the whole wide world the truth.

I had no idea that the journey toward uncovering the truth was far more difficult than I could've ever imagined, especially when I was awakened that morning, just moments after closing my eyes. "Knock, knock, knock, and knock." I heard the knocking, but it wasn't that loud. I thought it was down the road, next door, or noise passing by. Who would've thought that one of the biggest moments of my life was outside my door?

I continued to hear the knock, so I walked to the door, catching a feeling of fear as the noise coming from the door got louder and louder. It felt like getting a phone call in the middle of the night with a person you haven't spoken to for months on your caller ID. What was so important for someone to show up at this time of the morning? My hands started shaking and my body trembled as I slowly opened the door. At that very moment, my life changed forever. I will never be the same person. I can never be who I was before it all. Every day I look in the mirror I see a new me. I can try to make sense of who I used to be or try to help you know of the old me. However, you may never understand how much change I have been through, until you read my story, from the very beginning where it all started.

CHAPTER 1

CHILDHOOD FLASHBACKS

I GREW UP IN A SMALL TOWN with a mother, father, sister, one stepbrother, and a sibling who lived down the road. As kids, my sister and I were the best of friends. My brothers and I didn't hang around much, but it was love every time we were around one another.

I can remember some things like it was yesterday.

As expected sometimes with girls, my sister and I were both spoiled. We were far from rich but my mom made sure we had lots of toys, bikes, a trampoline, electric scooters, swimming pools, kids' parties, and money to buy extra things at school.

All of these made us feel like the luckiest kids on earth. I was on top of the world and I had so much joy.

There was nothing I couldn't have. Being the youngest child, I got my way more with my parents. My mom seemed to cry if I was having a bad day. However, even though I loved my mom and she loved me unconditionally, I was daddy's girl. When my dad left me at home, I would cry my little heart out, mad at the world. There was nothing anybody could do to stop me from crying.

One day, my sister and I came home from school and found that my dad's car was in the yard. It was quite unusual for him to be home so early. When we arrived inside, we found that our dear dad was in bed sick. All of a sudden, he could no longer work. My mom took on the role of working to provide while my dad stayed home. He would clean the house and cook for us daily. I can just remember him getting up to walk my sister and me to school every morning. He would teach us how to watch out for cars before crossing the street, and sometimes, my sister and I would mimic his words saying, "Watch out for them cars before crossing the street now."

Some mornings I didn't want to leave my room; all I wanted to do was watch my TV shows. I enjoyed watching Saved by the Bell. That show would make me want to skip school every time. The character Zack was the main reason I would always miss the school bus. Watching my favorite character just for a few minutes more was worth walking to school. It's amazing how someone we don't know and never even met can make us laugh and feel loved. I can still remember his pretty blonde hair and hazel eyes. He was such a lady's man who had me crushing in real life. I used to watch cartoon shows such as Scooby-Doo, Rugrats, Power Rangers, Cat in the Hat, SpongeBob SquarePants, The Proud Family, Blues Clues, The Magic School Bus, and Spider-Man.

As I look back on my childhood, I must say that I had many good days, but I experienced a shocking reality of life and death at a young age. It all started at the age of ten. I was walking around town with my cousin Ashley. Then I got a phone call telling me to come home. Ashley and her brother began to walk me home. We all were quiet the whole time we were walking. It felt so strange to get a phone call to come home in the middle of being with family. The closer and closer we got to the house, the more I could just feel my heart beating fast. I just knew something was wrong. Once we were on the road that led to my house, my arms began to shake. There was a tight pressure in my chest. Then my eyes fell upon blue lights flashing from the police cars, and my ears picked up on the screams coming from my family and friends. I didn't know what to think about the chaos; I was consumed with disbelief and mortified with grief.

Before I could even open my mouth, I heard my uncle say, "Oh no! My brother. . .not my brother." I knew then that something had happened to my dad. I was not sure what was going on, but I knew that it was nothing good. When I looked around, I saw people going into the house looking forlorn, so I began to walk into the house too. Just then the police grabbed my hand and told me I couldn't go in.

"That's my dad. I'm going in," I replied.

As I snatched my hand away from him in anger, I poked my head through the door, and there I saw my dad dead on the living room floor with a cigarette in his hand. I felt as if my heart had jumped out of my body. I started screaming, crying, and running in circles.

"What happened to my dad? What happened to him?"

No one answered me, no one! Tears fell down from my eyes in torrents as I mumbled inaudibly. My mother ran to hold me and all she could say to me was "It's going to be OK; just pray." That wasn't enough. I was lost in her arms. I was confused within my spirit. Then I heard the police say, "We are waiting on them to carry his body away." Moments later, men started coming into the house. As I stared at the two men taking my dad out of the house, I noticed my dad's facial expression. It appeared as if he was sleeping, but I knew that was not the case. He had on a white tee-shirt and some blue jean pants. They threw a white sheet over his body and began to put his body in the black bag. I remember one guy tripping over my dad and telling the other man that his body was heavy. I couldn't believe this was happening. He was being carried away. Everybody else that went away in a black bag never came back. How could my dad possibly come back from the black bag if no one else did? I just wanted to talk to him one last time. I couldn't! My dad was gone with no words of good-bye, no see you later, no more dad conversations; he was just dead.

From that moment, right then and there, I lost a part of me. I was heartbroken. I was losing sleep and I barely could eat. As

I was crying, I noticed that my mom wasn't taking my dad's death like I thought she should have.

"Mom, why are you not crying?" I asked.

"Baby girl, I must be strong for you and your sister. I must be strong for myself. Some hurt you just can't express and one day you will understand." She took me with her the next day to make funeral arrangements.

As the weekend approached, we prepared for my dad's funeral. I met his sisters, brothers, and a lot of his cousins whom I never knew. For some reason my dad's family and my mom's family never got along.

On the day of my father's funeral, I recall my uncle yelling, "You killed him, you killed my brother," blaming my mother in front of everyone. He thought she had something to do with my father's death. My aunt didn't like the fact that my uncle was accusing my mother of murder. So, the argument between the two ensued, slowly increasing the disrespect I felt toward them at my father's funeral.

Meanwhile, my sister and I sang "Can't Give Up Now" by Curtis Burrell at the funeral. While singing, my face became red, my nose began to run, and I started crying with the microphone still in my hand. My sister then continued to finish the song by herself. My aunt stood there with us holding me and telling me everything was going to be all right, as tears continued to fall down my face.

As the hours passed and the days turned into weeks, I started to miss my dad. I didn't know how to express how I felt. I began to write my first poem to my dad at the age of 10.

I said to him:

"Dad, I Miss You!

My heart was broken when you went away.

Now I feel heartbroken every day.

I wanted you to remain with me.

I cannot see you, but I know you can see me.

I miss you a lot and I know you miss me.

We did not even get a chance to say our good-byes,
which brings tears to my eyes.

I just want to cry,

I miss you.

All the times we used to spend together

We used to play around and have some fun

Now that you are gone, the things we did
don't feel like we've done.

You were so close to me.

Taking you away was like showing me things
that I don't want to see.

If only love was the key.

I'll have you right next to me.

If I could fly like a bee.

You'll have so many gifts to receive.

Now all that I wish did not come true.

All I have is special memories

I miss you

Our love was so close and only God knows just how true."

(Original words written at age 10)

My mother told me that my dad died from a massive heart attack and I believed her, even when I was too young to know what that meant. After his death, I had no understanding. In my head, I felt his sickness was something he should have overcome. With my mom now working more hours to pay the bills, I felt isolated and uncared for. I stopped eating, had no friends, and I just wanted my life to be over. In losing my dad, I felt like I had lost a sister too. Growing up, my sister and I used to play hide-and-go-seek together, jumping on the trampoline, playing with the water hose and tickling each other non-stop. When my dad died, we began to grow apart. She started hanging with friends her own age. She would leave me at home while going to the store. It was common for me to go with her, but she didn't want to be seen with me around her new friends. I became just blood. I was then too young to be around my own sister. It was at this time that I began to write in my journal. Writing was the only way I could express myself. It made me feel free.

Since I was eight years old, I always wanted to get married, have a dream wedding, buy my dream house and my dream car, have kids, and live happily ever after. I thought it would be as easy as it sounded, but Dad's death made me see that we don't always get what we wish for. My dad walking me down the aisle would never happen. My mother was all I had left.

As life continued, I started making plans to do something with myself. I went from being born, being a toddler, child, teenager, to being a high school senior. I started to think about how I would survive being out on my own. I began to think about things like "What kind of job do I want?" "What kind of career do I need?" I couldn't depend on my mother to take care of me. Since Dad died, our mother had been paying all the bills by herself. She spent so much time providing for us that I don't think she ever grieved the way she needed to. The last thing I wanted was to make things harder for her.

I remember visiting my grandmother when she was in the hospital. I also visited my aunt in the nursing home. I used to assist with feeding, changing her clothes, and washing her face and hands. So, I decided to go into the healthcare field as a caregiver, a nurse, and work my way up to management. I was determined to succeed in life. I started college and worked toward my goals. I even got a job to help bring in some income. When my mother found out about my job, she smiled saying, "Welcome to adulthood with responsibilities." We both laughed aloud, happily.

CHAPTER 2

FALLING IN AND OUT OF LOVE

MARCH 2012, I HAD BEEN seeing this same man come inside the mall to eat and drink his coffee. He was very tall, dark, and surprisingly stocky looking. My heart fluttered over his almond-brown eyes and one could easily get lost inside of them. He wasn't my dream type, but I found him very attractive. Every time I saw him, he was alone.

One day, he caught me on my lunch break in the line behind him. As soon as he was checking out, I walked to put my food on the counter. "Are you going to buy my food too?" I said to him.

Looking at me, smirking, he said, "You got a job."

I just threw my food beside his items, assuming the cashier would scan everything, while blushing his way. I was a bit shamefaced when my classmate, Kera, who was working at the time, skipped over my items. Even when I asked her to scan my food, she refused. Just when I was removing my items, the guy then looked at Kera and said, "Go ahead, I will buy her food this time."

I felt some jealousy coming from her, but I didn't care. At the time, I was just ready to eat. I couldn't understand her attitude. As I walked to my vehicle, I heard this same man yelling, "Hey, Ms. Lady, what's your name?"

"My name is Hope," I replied.

I remember thinking to myself, "The first time I meet a guy I want to talk to, I am caught driving the worst car ever." The car was literally on its last legs making terrible sounds.

As he continued to approach me, I immediately told him that my car was in the shop and I was borrowing my mom's car to get to work and back. He just said, "Okay." He didn't care.

"So, what's your name stranger?" I smirked, while looking at him.

"My name is Thomas."

While we continued to talk, I asked him, "Do you have a girlfriend?"

"No, do you have a boyfriend?"

"Maybe," I said. "Do you have kids?"

He shook his head from side to side, in objection.

I went ahead to exchange numbers with him and afterwards, we would talk for hours at a time. He would call me every morning and I would find that I had never laughed so much in my life. This man seemed to have everything I wanted a man to have. He had his own car, crib, and job, no kids, and was responsible. He could afford to take me out to places and have a good time.

We continued to talk and then one day, I needed to find a ride to go pick up my car. I had no idea who would take me. I just knew I didn't trust my mom's car to go two hours away from town and back (I thought and talked about this aloud). Surprisingly, Thomas agreed to take me.

As agreed, he picked me up early Saturday (his day off). The entire drive we just talked a lot. I felt closer to him every time I heard his voice. We stopped at McDonald's on the way to get me a burger to hold me down until we picked a restaurant to go to. When we arrived at the shop to get my car, I paid over $4,000 for car repair. I was so mad and it was mostly because I never had to pay so much money. I wasn't used to responsibility, especially for a vehicle. After paying the clerk, the service tech led me to my car, and I immediately noticed the vent holders were falling out and one was even broken. After getting out of my car, I also noticed my windshield had a small crack. I refused to drive my car off the lot, so I left it there and demanded that they return my car to me just like it was when I'd brought it to the shop or better. I wasn't about to pay 4,000 dollars and allow them to make me fix something that happened on their watch. I was furious.

It was at this time that my male friend handed me some gum and told me chewing may help calm me. I looked at him like he was crazy (as if I could've kilt him with my eyes) because

I couldn't understand how gum was going to help me calm down. So, I just put the gum inside my purse. Then we left. When we got to the car, I got hungry again. The gum was the only thing close to a piece of candy that I had so I began to chew it.

As I began to chew the gum, I did feel more relaxed. He looked at me and said, "You seem calmer," and he blushed. He was right! I was so impressed because I never had someone notice the small things about me that I didn't even know myself. As we were driving back home, he asked to take me somewhere and I agreed. Ten minutes later, we pulled up to a place called Baskin-Robbins where I ordered strawberry ice cream. It was the best ice cream I had ever tasted.

This man was the man I had been waiting for all my life. He was not trying to buy me, and he pleased me with the simplest things like gum and ice cream. On the way back, I told him that I didn't want to go back home but wanted to spend the rest of my day with him. So, we went out to eat in his hometown, Down South. I was expecting to go to J. Alexander or Red Lobster because that's what I was used to, but we went to KFC. I ordered baked chicken, baked beans, mac and cheese, and a sweet tea. The food was good.

At that moment I knew that the amount of money didn't matter. I had never felt this happy. He thought I was shy at first but truthfully, I was just trying to go with the flow. I loved his swag. It was so different! After eating, he asked what I wanted to do. We both chose to go somewhere private to hang out. He asked if he could get a room since we had nowhere else to go and relax. I told him the only way I would get a room with him was if he promised to respect my body. He agreed! I took his pinky finger and there it was, our first pinky promise.

We drove around until we saw a decent-looking hotel room. After finding a hotel, he took his card and ID inside to pay for the room. Returning to the car with keys, he asked if I felt safe with him.

"Yes," I answered.

Immediately we got into the room, he turned on the TV, took off his shoes, and told me to relax. I soon found myself fast asleep in bed, tired from the long drive. At 11 pm, I woke up and caught him looking at me with an old kind of smile on his face, as if I were everything he desired.

"Can I hold you?" he asked me.

"Yes, I guess," I replied.

When his hands held me, I could see myself spending a lifetime being held like that. The feeling of his manly hands holding me tight and talking in my ear was indescribable. As we began to share personal life stories, he told me about how he went to prison at a young age and did over five years. I admit that it caught my attention but didn't scare me away. I wanted him to tell me more on his own time.

"Did it have to do with murder. . .rape?" I asked howbeit.

He said no, so I left it alone until he was ready to tell me more. We were not rushing into anything, but we were honest with each other.

As the sun rose, we both began to rouse from sleep. Lying beside this fine man who never touched my body inappropriately made me feel so respected.

"Do you need anything before we go?" he asked.

"I am hungry," I replied.

As he prepared to go to the store, I noticed that his pants were still on and it just endeared him to me. There is nothing more tempting than having a man honor his words. I couldn't help but think that I had finally found the man meant for me.

A few minutes later, he called me on the phone. "Breakfast is coming up!" he said laughing as he made his way back to the hotel. "Now how is this man going to get me some food when he didn't even ask me what I wanted to eat?" I pondered, thinking that he was going to bring back all the wrong stuff for me.

When he walked into the room, I was quite surprised when he came with a chicken biscuit, apples, orange juice, and grape and strawberry jelly. He said he wasn't sure which jelly I would like but he knew he couldn't go wrong with chicken and fruits. I said, "Right, and who don't drink orange juice." We both just laughed. At that moment, he said I became his girlfriend. So, he became my boyfriend and we continued to date.

The next day I got a call to come pick up my car. Thank God! I was going crazy without my own ride. Every weekend I looked forward to seeing Thomas; he would come to my job, walking around. This time of course, he and I would flirt openly. He would always come through my line no matter how long of a line I had. It was kind of cute. During my thirty-minute break, we would meet at the food gallery to eat Subway. I always ordered a pizza and he would order sub sandwiches.

Months went by and we became deeply involved with each other. One weekend, he asked me to visit him at his house and I agreed. I was nervous about it being my first time driving on the interstate. What a big thing to do, coming from a small town of two stores, right!

I gassed up, got my car checked, and started my mini road trip. He would call to check on me at intervals, while I was driving. Fortunately, I made it safely to his house and when I walked in the door, the fragrance from the candles hit my nose. It was alluring and I was impressed by the cleanliness and simplicity of his home. He had everything all together; it wasn't too much or too little. It was just right! I felt comfortable, so I kicked my shoes off, took off my pants, and jumped in his king-size bed. I began to smell the sheets; they were so fresh. As I looked up, he was gone out of the room. I heard water running. I guessed he was trying to freshen himself up. My nosey ears tuned in; I could hear him dropping the soap. I laughed aloud. "What's so funny?" he yelled.

"Nothing," I called out. I was positive he had no idea what I was laughing at, as the TV was also playing in the bedroom.

"Come here, Hope." He was calling me to come in the bathroom.

"OMG, what should I do?" I had not told him my secret at that point.

I walked tentatively to the bathroom and when he saw me, he could tell I was hiding something.

"What is wrong with you, are you okay, Hope?" he asked.

"I'm fine." I got in the tub with him.

At first, I was saying nothing and just looking. Then, we started bathing each other, washing each other's backs and splashing water in a playful way. When we were done, he got out of the tub, passing me a towel. As I wrapped the towel around me, he picked me up and carried me to the bedroom. With so much care, he laid me on top of the bed and asked if he had permission to kiss me.

"Yes," I replied softly, after some hesitation. In my head, I was thinking that a kiss wasn't harmful. It literally turned out to be anything but harmless.

He proceeded nibbling on my bottom lip, slowly, until I was pushing to deepen the kiss. He subsequently tongue-washed the inside of my mouth. I felt like I would swallow him whole. Then he pushed the towel up halfway toward my chest, exposing my body. He stared deeply into my eyes as he slid downward toward my thighs. It was as if he was daring me to stop him. Then he started to lick my thighs one after the other, giving each one equal attention. I was at a loss for what to do; I felt so amazing that I was conflicted. I started to push his head away and at the same time, I arched my back, pushing my honey pot towards him. I was moaning loudly, and he did not need anyone to tell him that I was enjoying it. I tried to run away, pushing my body against the walls. The sensation between my legs became too intense. He followed me and put me back on the bed, and then he continued to send fire to all my nerves with his tongue. My eyes became so big and my legs began to shake; it was as if my body was begging for release from the sensuous torture.

"Hold on, wait, I have to pee," I said, right in the middle of things.

He let me up and I ran to the restroom. I got to the toilet and couldn't pee for nothing in the world. He asked if I was all right, while looking confused.

"I don't know what happened. I thought I had to pee." I looked so lost.

"Are you sure you are all right?" he asked, visibly worried.

"Yes, I am," I replied. Then I looked up at him and told him my secret. "I am a virgin and when you asked to kiss me, I thought you meant only my lips. I'm a little embarrassed, that's all."

"What, are you serious, Hope? You are kidding me!" His eyes got so big, as he looked at me. We just lay in bed watching TV, but I could tell he was still very much puzzled.

Thirty minutes later, he started touching my thighs. I could feel the sexual tension between us reaching a crescendo. I touched his face, rubbing the hairs on his head; it was as if I could not get enough of him. He took a nipple in his mouth and suckled on it. My whole body was on fire and I began to wriggle with pleasure. I could feel the wetness between my legs, and I couldn't have known how swollen with pleasure my clitoris had become. He expertly knew I was ready for him and so, he reached to the side of his bed and grabbed a condom.

He looked at me and without his eyes leaving my face, he slid down my panties. I felt relaxed; just looking at his face made me feel like I was safe. Looking into one another's eyes, we began kissing. We were oblivious to the outside world and it was just the two of us. The kiss was more intense, as our lips locked with each other's.

"Do you want me to?" he asked, looking at me ever so tenderly.

I nodded. My body was ready. I had always anticipated this moment, even though I knew not when or with whom it would happen.

"You are the most beautiful girl I have ever seen," he said at the same time he teased the walls of my honey pot with his penis.

I didn't know what to expect, I only followed the desires of my body as I arched my back and pushed my cherry towards him. When he pushed into me, ever so softly, I felt a sharp pain that vibrated all over my body. I didn't know whether to scream, cry, or moan this time around. I felt pleasure and pain, as he pushed further into my wet and pulsating cherry. He was gentle as he slowly thrust into me, covering up the pain with so much pleasure. I could feel our legs touching one another as he moved up and down on top of me. I began hollering, moaning louder than the last time. With each stroke inside of me, I became connected to him. I couldn't explain how I was feeling, but I knew I was being thrown into another plane where only the two of us existed. I know he felt the same way, because his face had become changed in ecstasy and he was groaning. His body on me had become stiff and then he yelped, at the same time that my mind exploded into multicolored particles. It was all new to me, but I would later find out that it was a climax.

Once Thomas had gotten off me, he threw me a towel. I felt a trickle of blood running down my thighs and the bed sheets were stained red. I was ambushed with many emotions that had me in a state of confusion. All he could say was "I popped your cherry." He said this smiling with all thirty-two of his teeth showing. Internally, I felt like a new woman just blushing away.

The excitement was all over his face. I could just tell he was pleased. And so was I. We just lay down for the rest of the night, cuddling so closely in bed.

Spending nights with him during the weekends became routine for us. I stayed over at his house so much that we agreed for me to move in with him after I graduated. Graduation was right around the corner: May 13th.

After graduation, I put in my notice to leave work right after July 4th. I hated to quit during a busy period, so I picked a time I felt comfortable with. By August, I was living with my boyfriend. Every weekend we went out. We had fun going to the movies, out to different eating places, even took walks in the park, and had fish fries with friends. I finally felt like I had a place to call home. There was no drama at all. After a long time, I finally felt like I belonged. Who would have thought that trouble was coming to my paradise?

One day, while I was sitting beside him, his phone rang. Even though it was a bit late and he had told me not to say anything, I did not pry, because I wanted to trust him. When he hung up, we just continued from where we had stopped watching TV and talking to one another. I had no reason to question him about the call. Fifteen minutes later he asked if I was hungry and I replied in the affirmative. I guess by that time, he knew I was always down to eat something. He started putting on his clothes and then I asked him, "Where are you going?" "I am going to get us some pizza. You go on and rest in bed," he said.

When I heard the door close, I immediately got suspicious. I just felt something was wrong.

I watched him through the window and noticed he was already on his phone. Who could he be talking to? Why did he have to leave to call this person? Was this the same person he told me to be quiet for? Something did not add up and I was now determined for answers. Forty-five minutes later, he came home with two boxes of pizza. The pizza was cold.

"How far away is the pizza place?" I asked.

"Twenty minutes," he replied.

The pizza place was actually about fifteen minutes away. It was a fair enough answer, so I decided not to ask him any more questions. In the same moment, I knew the next time he answered his phone, I was not about to be quiet. If it was not about his job, why should I be quiet?

Almost immediately, his phone rang. He answered. It was his mother.

"Baby, did you buy us something to drink?" I deliberately asked.

"No, but there is a little juice left in the kitchen," he replied, and I heard his mother ask him, "Who was that?"

He said, "Nothing." I knew then at that point that his mother didn't even know me. How could his mother not know the person who had moved in with him and the person he claimed he wanted to be with for the rest of his life?

I didn't think things could get any worse, but it did, quickly!

Six months after making things official, I received an unknown call from a young lady asking me about my boyfriend. She wanted to know if I was in a relationship with Thomas. She even asked me if I lived with him and how long we had been talking. I was so confused.

"How did you get my number and why are you questioning me about my boyfriend? Why are you concerned about our home?" I managed to ask.

She hung up and I called Thomas immediately.

"That was my coworker playing on the phone and I will handle it," he said.

I wasn't quite sure what he meant by handling it. I waited on this woman to call me again, but she didn't.

I decided to be smarter and find out who this woman was. So, I waited until he was sound asleep to go through his phone. His coworker had just texted him a picture. As I began to open the image, I just knew she had sent him a picture of herself without her clothes on. While I waited on the picture to download, my fingers started to shake. Rage was already boiling inside of me as I waited; I never had an image download so slowly in my life. When the image opened, I became speechless. His coworker was sending a picture of an ultrasound and it came with a message saying that she was having their first child. I could not believe the betrayal, the deceit that I had been blind to. I was totally blindsided.

The way I felt, stumbling on this piece of news, was indescribable. Uncontrollable anger engulfed me and burst out like an inferno. I began to hit him with his phone and while I did this, I cursed him, with tears flowing down my face. In this moment, the pain I felt was just indescribable.

"Who in the world did you play me for? Am I the dumbest woman on earth?"

I started packing my bags as fast as I could, ignoring his weak attempt at giving me an explanation.

"Is it your baby or not? Boy, get up out of my face."

When he kept pleading, I turned abruptly and then asked him the question whose answer I did not really want to know.

Screaming, with my heart racing, I asked, "Tell me the truth; do not lie to me. Is it your baby or not Thomas?"

"Baby, I'm sorry. I only slept with her one time and the only reason we were keeping contact was to take a blood test to find out the truth."

He begged me to stay and he promised that he was no longer involved with her and I believed him. I wrestled with my mind, "Why would he ask me to live with him if he didn't love me?" It was clear to me that he loved me. I am the one he comes home to at night, not her, I told myself. I have the keys to his car and his home, and access to his accounts. How can this woman hold an important role in his life? I made the decision to make it work at all costs. No, I was not happy about it. I knew it would take some time to forgive him, but I was not ready to leave either. I had just moved in with him and was starting school soon. I kept thinking, "Who wants to go right back to their mom's house after leaving?" "Why should I let some no-good female stop the happiness inside my home?" I couldn't just start over. This man took my virginity; he had taken a part of me that I could never take back. We were meant to be together.

I forced myself to stay with him and moved past the situation at hand. He started going to work and coming straight home. Everything seemed normal again. This man was showing me he was trying to make us work. Even on weekends, he stayed around me. He used to go back home to visit his mother and stay all weekend. Having major trust issues made us both agree that he could visit his mom but could not spend nights. He would call and meet his mom for dinner from time to time but every night he was at home.

One day, he told me he had to go paint his mom's house. He said he was leaving Friday and coming back Sunday morning. I asked to go with him, but he said his mom wouldn't allow me to stay because she talked to his baby's mother a lot. Unbelievable! This man was playing my trust.

The coworker who may have been pregnant by him became his baby mother and the baby wasn't even born yet. Even his mother already recognized this woman as his baby's mother. Worse still, he was no longer coming home at night. The more I forgave him, the worse he became. He had no respect for me anymore and I was the last to notice.

Every weekend he would pack up his clothes and tell me he was going to stay with his mother. I used to believe that, but in time I would come to know what the truth was. While he was gone, I received another unknown call, only this time I heard him in the background arguing with the lady on the phone. This was the so-called coworker! I told her to put him on the phone and he was bold enough to say, "Hello." A part of me didn't even want to hear his voice inside of her house; I was devastated. I couldn't see myself living without him. I nearly begged him to leave her and come home. He said, "Okay," and hung up. While I stayed by my phone waiting on him to call me, I noticed that three hours had passed by. Not only was he not going to call, he ignored all my calls. I even tried calling him with a private number as if he didn't know it was me; I kept calling back to back. I was hoping that he would answer at least one of my calls. I even got my best friend to call him from her phone. I was so desperate, and I was irritated by my actions. How could I force a man to pick up his phone and talk to me? It was clear for me to see that he had no respect for my feelings at all.

Quickly, he went from cheating on me to hitting me and becoming very abusive. It even got to the point where I couldn't ask him anything about what he was doing. I remember busting out screaming, "That girl doesn't even love you. She's just using your dumb self for money." Like a loose cannon, he threw his phone at my face, causing me to bleed. I was bleeding badly and my right eye would not open. I couldn't believe it.

"You must love her more than you love me," I said, amidst crying. "You're the one cheating, not me, but you want to hit me. Really, Thomas?"

He just looked at me as if he was sorry but not sorry. He gave me the "deed is done" type of body language. From that day forward, I never saw the same man I had met. Gone was the kind man who cared a lot about me. He was gone and wasn't coming back.

Months turned into a year, which turned into three very long years of him playing games. He played with my heart, my emotions, and my being. How did I allow so much disrespect? When did I become immune to the extent of just accepting his behavior? Every time I said I would move out, he would laugh at me. I always wondered if he thought I was incapable of footing my own bills or that I was too in love with him to leave. I remember all the emotional abuse like it was yesterday. I remember, "Don't just grab on me. I don't like that," whenever I would try to grab his hand or try to touch the man I loved. I got pushed away. "Don't touch me, don't lay on me. You act like you are lonely," was all I got whenever I tried to come close.

One day, I woke up and told myself "No more!" No more was I going to allow myself to stay in this situation that made me feel lesser than myself. Besides, I had no more fight left in me to forgive him again and again and again. No more was I going to expose myself to physical abuse and mental torture. How I endured all of that, I could never tell. But when a girl says it is enough, it is ENOUGH!

CHAPTER 3

TWO DOORS OPEN

I COULDN'T BELIEVE HOW the tables turned when I decided I had enough. I was turned off completely. I began to realize what I wanted and knew he would never be the man for me. I began to plan my escape.

I found a job doing home healthcare. I was a caregiver assisting elders with daily living activities. I became so good at my job that my client hired me full time and I started to earn way more per hour than what I was used to. I received $13 per hour, whereas at my former job, I was only making $9.00. God blessed me with $4 more. I felt accomplished. I was planning to live on my own, so this was huge.

I opened my first savings account and even picked up another client who paid seventeen dollars per hour. After Thomas noticed that I was becoming independent, he started paying more attention to me. He began to care about my work schedule and if I were home thirty minutes late, he would ask me why I didn't call him. He began to show affection by hitting my butt cheeks and would even try to joke in bed when we watched TV. He had become a champion at mixed signals and it was so confusing.

Even though he was being nice, deep down I knew my relationship was in trouble. It was over between us two. My focus was on me; I needed to do something fun for a change. For years prior, I had been holed up in the house worried about things he was doing wrong. So, I decided to have a party with my friends and some classmates. I had seen this party bus on TV and it seemed like a lot of fun, so I started calling businesses that had party buses and checking the prices on them. The first company I called gave me a price and like always, I wanted to compare. I called another company and they gave me about the same price. I said to myself, let me just call one more company. The third company I called was busy. This guy told me he was in a meeting and he would return my call shortly. Fifteen to twenty minutes went by and I had just given up on his call. After all, I already had two quotes that were affordable.

I began to look online at pictures, but shortly past 6 pm, my phone started ringing. I answered, and it was a man calling back from the last company. When I heard his voice, he immediately had my attention. We got to talking about the number of people who would be on the bus.

"In all, I have no idea because I am doing a class thing and a lot of them have gone their separate ways since graduation," I told him.

"The bus is too big not to have more than two people," he replied.

"I have fun everywhere I go and can turn up by myself."

"Girl, you are so funny. You are cool people," he said.

"Well, you seem down to earth yourself," I told him.

We got to talking, introducing ourselves and what not. He said his name was Roam.

"Hope, where are you from?" he asked.

"I'm a country girl from down south in the delta," I replied, laughing.

"What made you call for a bus with only two people?" Roam continued to ask.

"Honestly, I haven't had fun in a long time, and I am home going through a lot. Man, I need some fun in my life. It's 2015 and I haven't been out much since 2013," I told him, even though I never met him before.

"It wasn't about my classmates. I just really needed to get out and do something different." We continued talking and the conversation just flowed; nothing seemed forced. This man was smooth, and I couldn't get over his voice. As we began to hang up the phone, he asked to meet up with me. I agreed!

I had no idea what this man was going to say next. I remember thinking, "He is bold." I also wondered if he was a serial killer, but I wasn't about to pass up on an opportunity to loosen up some. I agreed to meet him at a public restaurant in separate cars. I then got in the tub, put on a nice pink and white dress, and some heels that I could only walk halfway in.

He pulled up in a limousine at about 9 pm and I asked him, "Why did you come in your work vehicle?"

"Because I can do it like that," he said.

There was a moment of awkwardness because I was immediately put off by his cockiness, but he was so fine, so I forgave him quickly.

All I could see was his muscles working together to form his body, his mixed skin complexion, and his low haircut bringing out all his facial features.

He greeted me with a hug right before walking into the restaurant. Once we got to the table, we both ordered burgers (well done) and fries. We talked for hours until I realized this man could really run his mouth. We talked about our short-term goals, whereupon he told me about wanting to build his home, go on vacations, and just grow. In turn, I told him about my goals of becoming a business owner. He talked about his family and asked me several questions about mine. He nearly talked my ear off, but I enjoyed every word he said. It was fun hanging out with him.

When we were about to leave, I hugged him and began to get in my car, but he asked if I wanted to see the inside of the limo.

"No," I said.

"My boss is out of town and I have the limousine all night so it's fine," he told me.

I couldn't resist it, so I agreed to look inside. "Why is he being so unbelievably kind?" I wondered. My emotions were just overwhelmed, because I was not used to this kind of attention, especially in recent times. I said to myself, let me peek inside and go home before I do something I will regret. As I began to peek inside the limousine, Roam lightly pushed me in, so I could really see the inside of the limousine, and boy, was I impressed. The interior was quite romantic, with color-changing lights, nice wine glasses, balloons in red, black, and white (everybody knows red and black are my favorite colors), and the music playing was perfect R&B. This man knew just what to do to catch my eye. I had never experienced this type of stuff; it was like watching a movie where the couples ate on the roof of a building. This was far more than I had ever imagined. It wasn't all about the limousine but the determination to cater to me. "OMG, why is this man rubbing down my back like this?" I was fighting my desire for him, but I was losing that battle. All I could think about was the short time I'd known him. The music continued to play even louder as the songs changed and to hear ourselves, we had to whisper in each other's ear, making us quite close.

"Are you okay?" Roam asked.

I couldn't respond because all I felt was the warmness from his breath. I wanted to kiss him. I had never been in the presence of a man who seemed to care about everything about me. Sadly, the only man I had to compare him with was my current boyfriend, who had not called me all day. During this moment, everything felt beyond perfect. He continued to rub down my back, slowly. I could feel all ten of his nails lightly scratching different areas of my back. My body had chills and it wasn't from me being cold. The way that he caressed me sent sensations up my spine.

My heart fluttered as I began to become moist and open between my warm thighs. I felt like I had been in a Jacuzzi tub (fully relaxed). His lips left a trail of soft kisses leading up my neck. I had never been kissed on the back of my neck before like that. In my mind, I was like stop but my body wanted him to give me more. He went from the back of my neck to kissing down the left side of my arm, putting my fingers all in his mouth.

I then began to say, "No, stop, please stop." I got up and started to get out the limo, but he softly pushed me down. A part of me wanted to say no but a larger part of me couldn't find the will to object. As he was pushing me down, he began to kiss me on my mouth, and then touching my breast, even putting my nipples in his mouth. It was too much for me to say no again. I wanted him. I wanted his body, his mind, and his soul.

He took my panties off and began to go inside of me. I immediately stopped him and asked him if he had a condom. He told me, "No" and I started putting my clothes on in such a rush that he could tell I was serious. It was a major turn off. He then went to the front of the limousine and said he found one. Then I asked, "Do you walk around with condoms?" He replied, "No, but my boss makes employees keep them in here to give them out to customers. I forgot because I haven't had to use a condom in years due to my past commitment."

I believed him. To me, he seemed secure.

He took my panties back off, while he put on the condom. I became excited again as he got on top of me and slid inside my honey pot. The way that this man moved inside of me and the way that he touched me was like he was trying to snatch every feeling I ever had out of me. For the first time in years, I felt wanted. I no longer felt lonely. He was inside of me and so focused on just me. With every touch, he was patient and careful.

Afterwards, we looked at the time. It was 1 am and we were the only two vehicles out in the parking lot. I didn't even want to go back home. I didn't know how to go back home. I got in my car and five seconds after driving off, he called me to make sure I got home safely. He stayed on the phone with me until I was in the house with the doors locked. We said our goodnights.

The next morning, I woke up wondering what had gotten into me the night before. I was living with one man and having sex with another. I just knew I had started something that I had no solution for. Still I wanted to learn more about him. I was not ready to let that night be the last I saw of him. Before I could get up out the bed, I received a good morning text. It was from the new guy. I replied, "Good morning to you too." Then he asked me to meet him for breakfast. I woke up with my stomach growling, very hungry, so I didn't see the harm. I said, "Yes!"

When I got home from breakfast, Thomas was home. He didn't say a word to me about why he did not call or text me all weekend. He just went straight to the room and started watching Netflix and texting on his phone. For the first time, I didn't care.

"Why are you so happy?" he suddenly asked.

Surprised, I replied, "No reason."

I began to wear sexy lingerie around the house and was in good spirits. The good vibes were ricocheting off my skin. The entire time I was at home, I was having flashbacks of the moments I had with the other guy. Gone were the constant thoughts and worry about Thomas. Everything inside me wanted to be with this new guy. I wanted to feel important to someone again and Roam made me have all the feelings I was missing, especially the feeling of being loved. It wasn't long before I started making time for Roam.

Every day, I had to see him. We went on several dates and I even met his family. We attended several concerts, NBA games, and pool parties together. Being an older guy, he was full of fun and updated on everything. On one of such dates, I lost track of time and when I turned on my phone after a while, I noticed fifteen missed calls from Thomas. It was almost midnight. I rushed my clothes on and went home. I felt sick leaving Roam and I was so tired of sneaking around. When I got home, Thomas was in the bed asleep, so I just climbed in bed with him, but facing the opposite direction. He turned over and put his arms around me. I found it strange because he stopped showing me any affection months ago. Without any words, I just closed my eyes.

The next morning, Thomas asked me where I was the other night.

"No, where do you go every weekend is the right question!" I replied.

We both walked off and the conversation was over.

He would walk around the house looking at me as if he knew I was cheating on him. I was not only cheating but I had found love. I was sick and tired of not waking up next to the man I loved, and I just couldn't continue to keep both doors open. The weekend came and like always, Thomas was gone. I was fed up and that was the last straw for me. I packed my bags and took everything that I owned. I moved completely out without warning. I didn't even leave a letter behind. Finally, there was no more hiding or leaving before the next day. Roam had me all to himself.

Moving in with Roam made me feel empowered. I finally gained the strength to walk away. I never wanted to break up with Thomas. Instead, I wanted him to choose me and rebuild our relationship. It dawned on me that it was never going to happen. Finally, I was done and ready for my life with Roam.

CHAPTER 4

WHO DO I CHOOSE?

T HE NEXT MORNING WAS a quick jolt to my new reality. I was still in disbelief about how my life had changed overnight. I now woke up to my new boyfriend cooking breakfast, hugging, kissing me, and showing me all the affection I begged Thomas for. Roam slowly painted a new picture for me. I no longer had to beg for affection; instead, Roam would always urge me for a touch. I was considered in everything and every time we were out, I was respected and cherished. My best moments were with him; I had my first vacation and flew on a plane for the first time in my life, with him. He introduced me to wine, luxurious soaks in bathtubs, makeup sessions at luxury makeup stores like Macy's, and endless shopping.

I felt myself falling in love fast, deep, and quickly, but I was a happy, contented woman.

One day while we were on a vacation, he took me to Macy's for a makeover. Afterward, he told me to dress up in heels and something sexy, because he had a surprise for me. After rummaging in my wardrobe, I settled on a white dress, which was covered with white flower designs from top to bottom. It wasn't too long or too short and my body fitted right into it, just perfect. I grabbed my silver diamond heels from Macy's and I was all ready for the surprise Roam had planned. I walked down to the first floor, and I noticed Roam looking at me like he never had before, while standing there in an all-white suit. He was so fine, and I almost thought for a second that we were going to get married. All we were missing were rings.

After driving twenty-five miles out, we pulled up to this place. It had so much water that I assumed he wanted us to chill at a beach. We both got out of the car and walked towards the water, on which I could see two gigantic ships. Impressive!

"I scheduled for us a 4-hour dinner cruise and hired a photographer to capture every moment," Roam whispered in my ear. I replied with a smile and a kiss on his forehead.

We boarded the ship and prepared to eat dinner. When the food came, it was so good and was accompanied by a delicious dessert. The music played as we chilled near the water, looking up at the sky. There were no stars to view, but the weather and mood were perfect. Later that night we just held each other until we fell asleep. It was a great climax to a beautiful vacation.

Upon returning back home, I felt sick. At first, I thought it was probably a bad landing after eating a full breakfast, but after a week of being at home and still feeling sick, I knew there was cause for worry. I had started to feel dizzy and nauseated. So I told Roam about it, but he didn't take me seriously, so I went ahead and scheduled an appointment with my doctor. After collecting my urine, the doctor told me that I was 3 months pregnant. Three months ago, I was still living with Thomas and had just begun a relationship with Roam. It was by far the worse situation I had gotten myself into.

"What am I going to do now? I can't win for losing. How will I break the news to my new boyfriend? I don't even know which man is the father." These thoughts danced in my head, throwing me into a state of chaos.

When I broke the news to Roam, it turned out that he had some health issues; hence his chances of being the father were slim to none. He asked that I withhold this information and told me that he would raise my child as his own. I just couldn't keep this information from him. My ex-boyfriend and I had been trying for years to have a baby and so I felt that it was a sign to get back with him. I met with Thomas and told him about the baby.

He immediately wanted me to move back with him. He told me that he was sorry for pushing me away. I believed that he had finally gotten my point. I thought that after I had proved to Thomas that I would leave, he'd act better toward me. I don't know what it was, but I had waited on things to be how they used to be for a long time now. The right thing to do was to allow him a chance to be a great father to our child. I didn't want to separate my family. I broke the hardest news ever to my new boyfriend. I went home, and Roam was in the living room playing his game. I told him we needed to talk more. He looked at me like he knew it was coming.

"Are you and Thomas getting back together?" he asked.

I didn't want to tell him that, but I had to be honest with him. I was hurt looking into his eyes and telling him that I was moving back for the betterment of my child. The next day, I moved back with my ex. I thought things were finally on the right track. I thought we could just pick up the pieces. That was until I realized I had a major problem. I was no longer in love with him. I had given my heart to Roam, the man I had just told I didn't want to be with.

During this time, Thomas tried to be affectionate and to be a new guy, but it was hard to forget all the years of abuse and disrespect. Besides, the only man I could think of was Roam. About one week after moving back in with my ex-boyfriend I went to the doctor and found out I was having an ectopic pregnancy. I had to have an emergency surgery to get my egg removed. The doctor said there was no way my pregnancy would end successfully. The clinic wanted to schedule my surgery within 48 hours to prevent further damage to my organs. No one else even knew I was pregnant because I was just coping with the news myself. I had to not only call my family to tell them about the baby, I also had to tell them about the surgery that was scheduled to remove the baby. What's more? I would have to explain to them why two men would be present. How embarrassing! My life was a bit too much for me and I knew it would be too much for my mom. Regardless, I knew everyone had my back.

My surgery was successful and when I woke up, I couldn't understand what the doctor was saying because I was so drugged. I remember waking up after falling back into sleep and seeing Roam, Thomas, and my mother in the room. I had to use the restroom, but I was in too much pain to walk. The nurse came in the room and told me I had to get up and walk some so I could go home. I thought she sounded crazy. How could I go home with cuts on both sides of my stomach?

Roam said, "Call me if you want me to come pick you up or if you need anything." I looked at Thomas, saying nothing to Roam, I just knew they both were respecting my mother being present. Watching Roam walk out of the room was hard. I wanted to go with him so bad. I couldn't. My mother had her bags over at Thomas' house and we had already made plans to stay with him. Over the years my mother and Roam had talked many times. She knew him as my boyfriend, but she didn't know half the stuff that was going on. When we got to Thomas' house, he was overboard nice. He cooked for me and my mother and I never had to worry about breakfast, lunch, or dinner. If it was something my stomach would allow me to eat, he would cook it. I found myself having KFC (baked chicken and potatoes) daily. For some reason, I couldn't keep anything else down. While Thomas went to work, my mother would help walk me to the restroom and gave me my medicine. I was in so much pain that I began taking my pain pills back to back. Instead of every six hours, I took them every three to four hours.

During my recovery, Thomas was overly nice and caring, so much so that I began to think that maybe Thomas was the one. Perhaps we just had a bad time in our relationship, I reasoned. I decided to just forget about Roam, because I felt it wasn't fair to Thomas or me. I put Roam on block as a result.

After my mom went back home, Thomas and I had a serious talk. His baby was on the way and the lady had threatened him with child support if he didn't leave me. He was all right with paying the money and we also agreed to be fully involved in the child's life. After just losing a part of me, I didn't mind being a stepmother.

A couple weeks later, I was totally blindsided. Thomas' baby mother became homeless and I was told to move out. He said that she needed a place to stay.

"It hasn't been a week since my surgery. Where am I supposed to go?" I asked.

"Get you an apartment and I will help pay rent."

"How am I going to get an apartment overnight and you want me gone this week? I don't even have a job right now. It would take weeks to search for a place I am comfortable with," I protested.

We just left the conversation alone.

The weekend came and once again, Thomas was gone. He didn't come home Friday night or Saturday night. Sunday morning, I unblocked Roam and called to apologize. I asked him if I could move back with him after I explained that the baby was the only reason I was trying to work things out, which was the truth anyway. He told me I could move back. I packed all my clothes and never went back to Thomas' house again. Later that night, Thomas would call to ask why I had left, but I was so done. Although I realized I was in love with them both for different reasons, I couldn't bear hurting Roam anymore. Besides, I was tired of the back and forth. My choice was made.

It took Roam and I a few months to get back on track. I could tell he had lost a little respect for me. In his eyes, he was always second choice but that was far from the truth. When things calmed down, I asked him to have a baby with me. After losing a child, I needed to be a mother again. We even talked about marriage. I scheduled a normal check up to start preparing for another child. This time, I was ready to pick up the pieces and start a new life with the man I loved and who loved me just as much. I could only hope for the odds to be in our favor.

CHAPTER 5

ROUTINE CHECK UP & RESULTS

I WOKE UP ON AUGUST 4, to a covered food tray with toast, omelet, bacon, grits, hash brown casserole, and a glass each of milk and orange juice. My boyfriend cooked me breakfast in bed; it was definitely something I could get used to. After devouring all of that, I was so full that I just wanted to fall into bed and sleep, but I had a doctor's appointment to get to.

Upon arrival, I requested to receive tests for HIV, herpes, and other STDs. All I wanted to do was confirm what I already thought I knew. I wasn't worried at all. I was preparing for my future. Lines had begun to fall into pleasant places for me; my career at this point was going great and three days prior, I paid my first month's rent on the office building for my company. I had worked my way up from getting paid $9 to $13, and as high as $22 per hour. I was in very high spirits. Everything was starting to look up for me.

I was sent to the phlebotomist to have my blood drawn and after that, a colleague brought me some food to get my energy up. Everything was good.

On August 10th, I saw a missed phone call at work and when I called the number back, it was my doctor's assistant. She told me that my doctor wanted to see me as soon as possible.

"We have an opening today around 4 pm, can you come?" she asked.

Although I had to be at an event at 6 pm, I agreed to stop by the clinic first. I then called one of my caregivers to come relieve me from work. When she arrived, I told her I had to go back to the doctor because something was abnormal and I didn't know what. The twenty minutes' drive to the clinic had me thinking my other ovary was messed up. I remember getting irritated waiting in the waiting room. I remember feeling like something more was up. Why couldn't they just tell me that over the phone? Why make me drive all the way up here? These people didn't consider the other party when it came to time, I thought. Finally, they called my name. I walked in the room and waited on the doctor. About fifteen minutes later I heard a knock on the door and the doctor walked in. I stood up then, ready to leave because my time had been wasted.

"Hello, Ms. Hope! I called you in because I wouldn't feel right telling you this over the phone. Would you sit down please so we can talk?" she said as she walked into the room. Then she gave me this look as if she wanted to cry. She knew all about my career, my business, and me preparing for another baby, so I was worried.

"Is everything all right with my test?" I asked.

"Do you want the bad news first or the good news?" she asked.

I said to her, "Give me the bad news. I'm used to it."

She began to drop her head slightly. The next words that came out of her mouth were, "I'm sorry to inform you but your test results came back and you are HIV POSITIVE!"

I turned my entire face toward her and said, "EXCUSE ME, I'm what?" I just stared at her with my eyes in wonderland, as if I were daydreaming. "What in the world, what good news can possibly be in the same life as HIV positive?" I thought silently.

I just knew it had to be a mistake. "Are you sure? Can we retake the test?" My voice began to shake as I tried to convince the doctor that she was wrong, and some huge mistake had happened with my results. In denial, indeed, I was.

"We have to send you to the health department, and they will do the final confirmation. I couldn't tell you this over the phone. I'm sorry!" the doctor explained.

"It's okay, I'm sure this is a mistake, trust me," I replied with confidence.

The doctor looked at me, with her eyes looking straight into my eyes, and grabbing my right hand, she told me that her test showed repeated reactions to the virus and she was almost sure I had HIV. It was just routine to send patients to the health department for final confirmation. My mouth was wide open and my eyebrows were raised so high; I couldn't believe it.

"Oh noo, oh noo, no hold on, wait…somebody help me, please. I need help. Tell me it is not so." I started crying as I dropped to the floor. The chair I was sitting on was now sitting on me.

Devastated, my whole world came crashing down, and into the abyss was where my soul was thrown. I was screaming aloud, "I am going to die." I tried standing up to only fall back down. The doctor called for assistance as I started hitting the walls and throwing to the floor every piece of equipment that I could put my hands on. "Why me, why…?" Life meant nothing to me anymore. I just knew my time on earth was coming to an end. My head was spinning so fast, I couldn't process all this. "Am I going through this? Am I HIV positive? Are you sure, Doc? Please tell me something different. Tell me you were just playing. Tell me something." I screamed, feeling so wretched. I watched my life end right before my eyes. I wasn't as familiar with HIV. I couldn't help but wonder how long I had left to live.

"Help me! God! Why me, Lord? Why me?" I screamed aloud. "Doctor please, am I that bad? If hell is real then I must've hit it head on. Must I die this way though? Will God ever accept me into those golden gates? Here I am, God. I am sorry, Father!"

The doctor tried to comfort me as she focused on all the positive things. She told me that HIV was **not a death sentence anymore.** At this very moment, I couldn't understand.

I was crying and talking at the same time. "How bad can life be? How low can I fall? I almost had it all, or what I thought was all. Yet, I ran into a brick wall. Now I am down on my knees. All I have left to do is face the truth or hide this for the rest of my life."

I was fumbling over my own words and speaking to myself. I began to pray in the doctor's office aloud. As I dropped to my knees, backup entered the room, but I heard the doctor say, "Let her finish her prayer." So, I continued praying aloud, saying,

"God,

I've been so wrong and made countless mistakes.

I've ignored all the warning signs you sent me,

Thinking I had full control of the outcome.

Lord, I now see that I don't have all the answers.

I know that only you can help me.

So I come to you, Lord.

I come to you as humbled as I know how.

I ask that you come see about me.

Come check on your baby girl.

Come into my world.

God touch my life.

Help me find my purpose.

Lord, I know I have been sinning on top of sins.

I slept with people I shouldn't have.

Lord, have mercy on me.

Say it's done.

I believe as you speak, it is done.

As you pour mercy over me, I accept.

I open my heart to you.

It's not that I don't have a choice.

I just believe in only you, Father.

I confess my sins with my own voice.

Forgive me, God.

I repent!"

Right after I got done praying, the doctor proceeded to give me my test results. "You haven't ovulated in months but you can still have a baby; I can help you with that," said the doctor.

"Are you kidding me? I don't even want my boyfriend anymore. How then can I want a baby? I could possibly have HIV! Can I go now?" The doctor then told me if I had any questions to call her, but for now she had to contact the health department. She asked if I had any thoughts of hurting myself or anyone else, and I said, "NO."

I left the women's clinic feeling horrible, slamming the door as I walked out. I was at the worse place in my life. Everything in my life was changing. I couldn't stand up or walk the same way. Mentally, I was dying, physically, emotionally, and spiritually with no willpower left inside of me.

I remember thinking back on abnormal changes in my body that I had ignored. I had a mouth ulcer inside my bottom lip, a small painless lump behind my ear, a sore throat, whole-body sweating, and flu-like symptoms. Although all my symptoms didn't show up at once, I brushed them off. I didn't think it was anything major. After a day or two, I would say, if it doesn't go away then I will go to the doctor. After two to three days, my symptoms would disappear. I did experience headaches but who doesn't? When I Googled the symptoms of HIV after I left the clinic, I was in disbelief. Almost all the symptoms I had been having were a part of this virus. I remember thinking, "All the times I was told never to completely trust Google, how can my symptoms and diagnosis be right?"

Later that day I called Thomas asking him to meet me. He was the first person I ran to because he knew me better than anyone. We agreed to meet outside his house. I could barely open my mouth when saying, "Please don't overreact, I must tell you something very important."

He said, "Whatever it is, it can't be that bad."

"It's bad; it is the worst thing ever," I replied. "I just left the doctor's office and I could be HIV positive. I have to go to the health department for further testing."

I was in tears, "Promise me, Thomas, that you will be here for me and we will work this out together."

"Whatever it is, I promise you that I am here," Thomas replied. His eyes were big and teary, but he seemed to have my back. He held me while I burst into tears on his chest. We both had been having sex with someone else so neither one of us could point the finger. Deep inside, I just knew Thomas had got this virus from the so-called coworker he was sleeping with. I couldn't believe I was in this mess. All I wanted was a faithful man to love me. I couldn't help but be mad at Thomas for sleeping around. All I wanted was for him to act right. Why did his baby mother or Roam even had to be involved at all? Why were we even going through this?

When I left Thomas' house, I proceeded to call Roam and stopped by his home, but no one came to the door. The next morning, I went to the health department and signed in. Moments later I was called to go to the back to give a blood sample. They were once again testing for HIV and STDs. They also wanted to check my CD4 count and to see if I had copies of the virus in my blood. They told me it would take at least a week or two to hear something back. Why don't they just let it be?, I wondered. I became overwhelmed with stress as I waited on my final results to come in. I tried reaching Roam to update him, but he stopped answering my phone calls. He was never at home when I stopped by. I became more depressed than I had ever been. I started calling help lines to prevent me from harming myself. I was slowly falling apart. I needed someone to tell me, "It's going to be all right."

Suddenly, Roam turned his back on me. He didn't want to meet up with me, refused to hold me when I wanted to be held, and he even asked me to pay him to see me. Roam was a totally different breed. I just knew he was so mad at me. Thomas was also acting funny. He visited me once or twice but he wasn't there like I thought he should've been. I was left to depend on strangers and too afraid to involve people I knew. I joined an HIV site and noticed I didn't like the page, so I immediately cancelled my membership. I then paid another $29.95 to get on positvesingles.com. I enjoyed the people on this site off the top. I knew I was around some motivational people, so I began messaging those who had HIV. One man told me he had been living with HIV for over 20 years and was undetectable the entire time. He even had two children with his wife and all three of them were HIV negative. He sent me links to read about the new findings on HIV if a person was undetectable. I began to feel better. After being on the site for 5 hours, I took a break.

Ten pm finally came and it was time for me to go home. I got in my car and headed home. I was still bothered, and I wanted to talk with more people, so I tried logging back into my account, but I had forgotten my password that fast. By the time I reset my password it was midnight, and I was super tired. Just as I was about to end my night, I ran across a profile with no picture. It said, ROAMKNOWS. ROAM was the name of my boyfriend. It raised my eyebrows for sure. I felt like someone was trying to warn me and everyone else. I was so not prepared for what happened next as I kept scrolling down the home page. I saw, ROAM! OMG! WOW! NO! As I focused in on the name that I already saw clearly, I dropped my phone, overloaded with shock. My boyfriend had his picture, his email, and his status showing that he lived with HIV. The status said he hadn't logged in for over a month, meaning that he was logged in 4-7 weeks ago at least. It was as if the universe wanted me to know. I cried all night. I couldn't talk, couldn't walk, my body was shaking, and my heart was racing. I felt so helpless. It was as if I was stabbed in the chest, shot in the head, and left to die. I didn't sleep that night; I couldn't even if I wanted to. He knew before me. He knew! What excuse could he possibly have? He was actively on a dating site for people living with HIV. I just never would've guessed that he knew and didn't tell me. Does it make him guilty of giving me HIV? I thought. No. Still, I felt betrayed by not only Thomas but Roam too. Roam knew weeks before me and for weeks now we had been intimate. I began to write my feelings down. Writing was always my go-to for pain relief.

I began to write without thinking:

"I Never Guessed You"

"I always knew there was somebody out there ready to break my heart.

Doing their best to pull me from the light into the dark.

Though I never guessed you.

I thought this you would never do.

I was wrong, but you were right.

Why didn't I believe the things I saw in sight?

I never guessed you.

You were someone I never thought to put a guess to.

Now you have done the things I never thought that you would do.

Why it's a person who got my heart in his hands?

So, that way it falls wherever he lets it land.

I just never guessed you.

Which is something I will always regret too."

After writing, I got in my feelings even more. My heart was breaking into a million pieces and I cried out loud, "I give up. I have no one. I am broken into pieces so tiny and there is no hope of mending. I can't continue with my life. I have no strength. I have no hope. I have no drive left in me."

It was hard to continue life like I had not just been shattered. I completely pushed all my friends away. I ignored all personal and business calls and even avoided talking to my mom. My life was falling apart, but the only thing I cared about was finding out who may have given me HIV.

After two weeks of wondering what was next, I got a phone call to return to the clinic. Still, there was no word from Roam. As soon as I hung the phone up, it started ringing again. It was Thomas.

"Did you find out anything yet?" he implored.

"I am headed to the health department now, but it is not looking good. If I was negative, they would've given my results on the phone," I replied. I then proceeded to tell him about the HIV site I caught Roam on. It still wasn't proof of where this HIV had come from, but I felt Thomas had a right to know.

"You are sleeping with this guy that gave us all HIV!" His voice had anger in it. "I am going to die because I trusted you. Stupidity! I should've known something wasn't right about that dude, he looks sick. Then you are lying to me about it."

"Tell me the truth!" he started to yell. "Tell me the truth!"

"If he had this virus, I didn't know, Thomas." The tears started to come. "I am just finding out and trying to see what is going on. All we can do is get tested."

"You might not even have it. I just didn't want to keep this a secret when this is serious. He could've gotten on the site after he found out just like I did. It doesn't mean he is the reason for all of this. Do everyone a favor and get a test before putting others in this?"

"Are you that in love and stupid?" Thomas yelled. He hung up the phone immediately. I was hurt but I couldn't blame him totally. I couldn't blame anyone because we all were sleeping with more than one person.

On my way to the health department for my results, I noticed Thomas calling me again.

"Hello, I am sorry to stress you, but this is hard on me too. Can we just work this out together?" I said to him, even before he could say a word. I thought he was calling back to be supportive.

"I am sitting here with my baby mother now and I told her everything. We want to know what is going on and you need to stop lying to me. You know whether you have HIV or not." The words were like hot, searing iron on my heart.

"Meet us up there at the clinic. Which clinic are you going too?"

The man that I thought had my back was teaming up against me. I hated that he told her. We did not even have all the facts, but he had gone ahead to tell the same person he knew hated me. Someone he knew that would tell others the first chance she got. I knew then that he was not team Hope. I told him to go get a test and to leave me alone.

"You are treating me like this when you know it could've been you who gave me this. How dare you?" I barked at him.

"Roam is the one on the HIV site, not me. You love him so much that he can't do no wrong. You need to open your eyes. This man is killing us all."

I finally arrived and walked into the clinic, shaken and ashamed. I felt like HIV was just written on my face; as if everybody in the building knew I had HIV and I couldn't do anything about it. I made my way up to the third floor and signed in. Twenty minutes later my name was called. I followed this woman to a room. She said, "My name is Mrs.

Perry and I will be giving you your test results today. Before I proceed, do you have any questions?" I said, "No, I don't." Then I heard her say, "You are HIV positive." I couldn't even cry anymore. I felt nothing. I just remember looking at her as if life was just over. I felt powerless, useless, and on the verge of suicide. I was smart enough to not inform her of what I was feeling. She proceeded to ask me questions about who I was involved sexually with. I wrote Roam and Thomas' names on the paper. I had to tell her how long I had been sexually involved with both partners. I wrote since 2012 for Thomas and 2015 for Roam. She asked me who did I think I got the virus from. I told her Thomas. She went ahead and informed me that it was her job to call the two people I had sex with.

"Oh noooo, my boyfriend is going to kill me," I told her. With an expressionless face she asked who my boyfriend was.

"I meant to say my former boyfriend is going to be so upset," I corrected my statement. "Which one do you think would be really upset?" she asked.

"Roam," I replied. "Roam has been nothing but good to me and I got him caught in this situation." She looked at me with confusion on her face. She explained that she wouldn't mention my name and how she was only allowed to inform my partners that they have been exposed to HIV and encourage them to make an appointment to get tested.

She continued to say, "Some people come in here and the person they got it from had it for years, but we are not allowed to say anything." She gave off nonverbal body language that indicated she wanted to say more to me but couldn't.

When she called both of my sex partners, Thomas didn't answer, and Roam hung up on her. I informed her that I had told them both about needing to get a HIV test and with a reassuring smile she told me to take one day at a time. I met with their social worker to sign up for medications. There, I went over programs that could help me pay for my medication with the personnel. It dawned on me then that this was not a dream I could wake up from; it was reality. I tried calling Thomas again, but his phone went straight to voicemail. It hurt me because I knew I would never have turned my back on him if the case was reversed. It was even sad to know that his baby mother had moved in with him; they were officially a family. I wasn't too mad about it because I knew she could never love him like I did. She was using him, and everybody could see it but him. I started to think about how blind Thomas was toward his relationship, while second guessing my own relationship with Roam.

Perhaps, I was truly blinded by Roam. He showed up and treated me good in ways I wanted from Thomas. Was Roam that good of a man or was he hiding the most unforgiveable secret? I was going to get to the bottom of it all. I didn't give myself HIV. It couldn't have been me. I was more hurt by the fact that I was probably the last person to know about this virus inside of me. I was hurt because whoever it was took away the chance to protect myself and watched me live every day without taking the right medications. Who did this to me? Who?

CHAPTER 6

VICTIM ALL OVER AGAIN

I Love You,

I love you more than love can love.

I want you more than want can want.

If you were in the air,

I'd jump for you higher than I ever jumped.

When I am on top of you,

I want to move like I never moved before.

I want to see you when I cannot see at all.

I want to feel you in my mind when my body no longer gets the urge.

I am ready to take that next step and yes, I have nerves.

Poem I wrote Roam when I first fell in love
(Sep. 2015)

After two years of dating Roam, I was stuck with so many mixed feelings. I knew only the truth could solve my problems. I decided to hire a private investigator. Roam was not talking to me, so there was no way to know anything. I wanted to know the exact day he found out. I wanted to understand how he could wait weeks trying to see how to tell me the bad news. HIV is very serious, especially going untreated. If he never cheated on me, maybe he thought my ex gave it to the both of us. I just needed to know more. Something about it all wasn't sitting well with me. It was something about the way the social worker had looked at me when I said he would be more upset. It was something about the way she had said that someone could have the virus for years and she couldn't tell me. It didn't feel like a random story; it felt like the legal way of telling me my story. Either way, I was determined to get to the bottom of it.

I walked into the investigator's office and asked if he could get me Roam's test results. The detective, Philip, agreed to investigate my situation. He told me the state paid him, so it was free of charge. All I had to do was sign a paper stating he gave me HIV without telling me his status. I signed the papers and left. Back at home, I was all alone with no one to talk to; my phone did not ring all day. I hadn't eaten and was barely getting sleep. I started watching a movie and ate some crackers. Then I tried to keep myself busy, but it didn't work. I started going through my phone, looking at pictures. All I could think about was Roam. Smiling at the pictures we took when we were out of town and having flashbacks of the moment in the hot tub when we ate pizza. I just needed to talk to him. I knew he wasn't going to pick up. I called anyway. Surprisingly, he answered. He came over to my house and lay around with me. We didn't do much talking and we didn't have sex. I just needed to have someone around. It became routine for us to hang out. Every day we would link up together. Every day I felt less pain. After weeks passed by, Roam and I were friends again. We agreed not to move too fast. He couldn't spend nights at my house per our rules, so I asked him to be gone before 10 pm. He left every night around 9 o'clock. Every night he would leave, I secretly wanted him to stay. I stayed up a few hours after he left, writing in my journal. I was finally starting to cope. Saying my prayers before going to bed every night, I could feel some joy coming back. That was until one morning when I woke up to a loud noise. "Knock, knock, knock, and knock." I heard the knocking, but it wasn't that loud. I thought it was down the road, next door, or noise passing by.

As I continued to hear the knock, I began to walk to the door, catching a feeling of fear. It felt like getting a phone call in the middle of the night with a person you haven't spoken to for months on your caller ID. What was so important for someone to show up at this time of the morning? My hands started shaking and my body trembled as I slowly opened the door. It was the private investigator that I had hired. Why was he here? What made him show up in person? I was apprehensive.

Waiting on him to speak, I just looked at him, wondering what now.

"I am sorry to inform you that your ex was diagnosed with HIV ten years prior to meeting you," he finally said and shattered what was left of my life.

I began to fall to my knees in total shock and suddenly I started to vomit. I couldn't believe HIV had arrived at my front door. My former lover gave me HIV and he knew he had the virus for ten years. All I kept thinking was, "Did he do this to me on purpose?" Did he even think for one second about my health? He never informed me even when I asked him about his status. I suddenly felt myself being pulled into a dark hole. Losing my balance, I stumbled, but the detective grabbed me with his hands, using the living room wall to keep me from falling. I was still crying when he guided me to a chair and gave me a tissue to wipe my tears. I wiped so aggressively; I was so angry inside. But the detective had been patient and considerate.

"Why are you so nice to me? This is not a part of your job."

"Somebody I know committed suicide when they found out they were HIV positive and that was the worst day of my life," the detective replied. There was silence.

"Yes, I was going to give you a call to let you know he had the virus since 2006 but something told me to come here in person," Detective Philip went on to say.

"Are you serious? I would've been fourteen or fifteen years old!" I felt so stupid.

Detective Phillip continued on, saying, "Just let me know how you wish to proceed. I will support you all the way through."

"I need time to think, but I will call you next week," I said with a cracking voice.

"It sounds great to me. I am here to help."

I couldn't talk any longer; all I did was rush the investigator out of my house. I wanted Roam dead and I wanted to kill him with my own hands. I wanted to hear him take his last breath, because I felt he was not worthy to live on earth. Ten plus years of not caring, of possibly spreading this deadly virus. I called Roam; he didn't answer. I left him a voicemail telling him what the investigator had found out. "I know you gave me HIV and you are going to jail. I hate you!" I yelled. Then I hung up the phone.

Less than a minute later, Roam called me and asked that we talk. I had no one else to talk to, so I needed him and a sense of reality. I wanted a listening ear. Even after everything that went down, I forgave him again for lying to me and giving me this virus. I still felt the need to have him around. The same person who hurt me the most was the same person I needed to comfort me at that time. I felt like I had no one else who could relate to me.

Later that day, Thomas' baby mother emailed me, telling me their results were negative. Immediately, Thomas cut off all communication with me. Roam was all I had. I knew if I pressed charges on Roam, he would go to jail, but how could I have the heart to do that? He was being very supportive.

On the day of my next doctor's appointment, Roam went with me and was there to help me pick out my medication. I was so preoccupied with HIV alone that I didn't have time to focus on why he didn't inform me. After the visit to the doctor, Roam and I went to a hotel room. He felt after all that had happened, we should be away from family and friends. I thought so too. We stayed in the room, watching TV and drinking wine. Later that night, we lay in bed together and my raging hormones were there to remind me that I had not been with anyone since I found out about my status. Besides, I was with a man I still loved; a man who I felt still loved me. A part of me was still in denial about him giving me the virus, but when he touched my body, I felt emptiness. I could no longer look into his eyes, or kiss his lips, or feel comfortable lying in the same bed as him. I found myself lying beside him wondering why and how. What led me to his bed once again? Why am I turning the other cheek? Is this logical? Love had me forgetting the unforgettable. Still, I yielded my body to him. Despite my raging emotions, my nipples still became taut when he kissed them. The inside of my vagina still became moist when he played with it, having two fingers strategically placed. The moan escaped my lips regardless of the confusion I felt.

I was in the middle of so many thoughts when he thrust inside me. Although I was mad at the nerve he had to use protection this time around, my honey pot still pulsated when he entered and welcomed his penis like it was home. While my body was reacting, my mind had frozen. It was like a nightmare as the first time I was told of my status began to replay in my mind's eye. All I could think about was the fact that he knew the entire time. Suddenly, I started to gag. I was disgusted and completely turned off. I could feel him pouring out his seed inside of me, even with a condom. When I looked up at him, I threw up all over the pillows. I wanted out of my own skin. I rushed into the tub, splashing my hands and finger scrubbing as hard as I could with the towel, trying to clean my body. No matter how much I scrubbed, I felt dirty. I didn't feel close to cleanliness. I began screaming with no words coming out. It was as though I was hurting so badly that I couldn't get the words out. That was when he rushed into the bathroom. With one look at me, he could tell I regretted sleeping with him again. He just made the bed and said nothing. I knew it was a huge mistake getting into his bed again; being intimate with him after everything made me feel like a victim all over again. When I got out of the tub, I went to sleep. There was nothing left to say.

The next morning, I told him that I couldn't be with him. I started to think about other girls he may have endangered. I knew I had to do something, if not for myself, then for others. I told him we could no longer see each other. I would only find out how vile he was two days after we had sex.

Two days after we had that disgusting sex, he sent me a video of him lying beside me after sex the other day. I had no clothes on in the video and it was obvious I was being blackmailed into silence. He tried to blackmail me with the video to stop me from pressing charges against him.

"If you are so sorry and innocent, why did you have sex with me again?" he asked.

I couldn't believe that I had been used again. He didn't come to me because he cared about me; he only wanted to get leverage and like a fool, I had fallen again. He did have a point, I thought. How could I sit in court calling him such a monster if I still slept with him? How could he be such an enemy if I still answered all his calls? It wasn't fair; I was confused, lost, and frustrated.

I needed some fresh air; it felt like my confusion was choking me. I got in my car and rode around for hours, driving with so much anger and frustration. Somehow, I found myself at the top of a residential building breathing deeply.

"Why me? Why, my God, have you given up on me? Am I not worthy of an answer, Father?" I mumbled to myself as I sat on the edge of the roof, rocking back and forth with the urge to leap. At that moment, I made the ultimate decision to end my life permanently. My silent torment had won me over. I became a creature of my own regrets and built-up sins. Wind whooshed past me as my fingers began to shake, anxiety kicking in, and my head began to spin. I closed my eyes after analyzing the only choices I felt I had. I continued thinking with my eyes closed, still rocking, and all of my cons outweighed my pros. As I stood up, an apex of fear rushed over me and my phone began to ring. I could feel my heart palpitating as I answered my phone. "Hello, are you there?" I remained on the phone, breathing heavily, placing myself in a sitting position on the roof. "This is Detective Philip. Ms. Hope, I was calling to check on you because God told me to do that. God is looking out for you and you have Him on your side. If you want to proceed with charges, you let me know. You have all the power inside of you because no matter what, God created you." Then the sun just started shining down on me, with a feeling of peace entering my heart. "He answered me," I said. He answered me! Detective Philip asked me what I was saying but I had no time to explain. I rushed him off the phone and assured him that I would be just fine. I felt something inside my body that I had been praying for. I felt like God had answered me. I was moments away from suicide, moments away from giving up, before the detective called me. I just knew it was meant to happen that way. I got down from the edge of the roof and I knew it was time to face whatever I had to face. I was no longer afraid to look Roam dead in the eye.

CHAPTER 7

AM I LIVING OR DYING?

I WAS DETERMINED TO GET my peace of mind back, so I researched other ways to cope mentally. My mind was still all over the place, but I knew I didn't want to trust Roam ever again. I would rather be stuck alone than be around a person who was constantly hiding the truth from me. While browsing online, I ran across this therapist's information, "If you need counseling regarding bad relationships, depression, low self-esteem, drugs, marriage issues, and more, contact Counselor Mitchell at 444-444-HELP. I hesitated to call this therapist. I remember thinking that I could handle my problems by myself, as I was shown growing up. Everything would get better with time, right? I told myself, "I don't have no mental health issues and there's nothing wrong with me." After wrestling with my mind, I came to terms with the fact that there was nothing wrong with seeking professional advice. There's nothing wrong with admitting that life gets too hard to bear such a heavy load of unexpected situations. Against all odds, which I'd known all my life, I called the number anyways to make an appointment. I was able to book an appointment in the same week, because somehow his assistant could tell that I was in desperate need.

Ten AM two days later, I arrived at Counselor Mitchell's office. Each session was essentially a problem-solving session. I described my situation, and my feelings about it, and then the therapist used his expertise to assist me in trying to resolve my problems.

At the beginning of a session, the therapist allowed me to share what was on my mind, and also asked what goals I had planned. I spoke openly and honestly because I felt comfortable. I had the ears of someone who was genuinely interested in my happiness. I was never criticized, interrupted, or judged as I spoke. It was totally confidential. In some sessions, I was given assignments and one of my activities included keeping a journal. There were sessions where I walked out, gave up, or got very frustrated and off track. It took the ugly truth to unwrap and release some hurt. I accepted being perfectly imperfect. Overall, counseling helped me a lot. I no longer felt like I needed a man to live my life. Things were changing and I finally felt that loving myself was just enough. I gained even more strength to face Roam and everything he had done to me.

For the first time since my results, I started dressing up nice, going out with my friends, and picking back up my normal routines. I would take hours out of my day to research HIV. It wasn't anything like I had imagined. When facing the truth, I realized that I was more hurt by the fact that he hid the secret from me more than catching HIV, especially when

I wasn't naïve to the risk of having unprotected sex. I trusted him with my life, and this is what I ended up with in return.

Although I was on my way to healing, I could not let Roam go free. He had no remorse and I knew that he would not think twice before infecting another unsuspecting girl. So, it was finally time to send Roam where I felt he belonged. What a bittersweet moment it was to sit there signing papers on the love of my life. I wrote my statement after discussing with the detective the kind of charges he would face. I never felt so confused in my life; I knew I couldn't let him get away with what he did and probably was still doing. Yet, I couldn't help but be burned at heart.

September 3rd, 2017, I chose to move forward with putting him behind bars. I chose to face him and let him know he was guilty as charged and at the very least, I was going to expose him. Yes, I knew he might try to come after me, my safety might have been compromised, but I felt it was worth it all. He was a man who had become different from what I knew and sometimes, I wondered if he had been any different or if I had been too blind to see.

"I Thought,

I thought I knew who's right for me.

I thought I saw all there is to see.

Well it's a lot that I don't know.

Everyday there's more and more.

I'm so tired of getting lied to.

Every other day the same lie is new.

I thought when bad times come, I'll know what to do.

Well, that's not true.

I thought I would never at this age go through the things I'm going through.

I thought the things I did, I'd never do.

Now wondering where in my life should I start, when constantly being broken is my heart.

Being with a person, but just not knowing who they are.

Having to reach out, but not knowing how far.

I thought I had your heart."

September 4th was a day I will never forget. It was the day I decided to tell my mom the truth about my health status. I just knew I would be a disappointment. I was her baby girl. All I ever wanted to do was make her proud. I never wanted to be the cause of her crying at night. How would I even start? "Mom, I have HIV?" Loudly, I practiced the words I was going to say. As the day passed by, I tried to find the right moment to talk to her, but there seemed never to be a right moment. I wanted her to have time to think. I also wanted her to just go to sleep without stressing.

"Mom, can we talk?" I said, two hours before her bedtime of 10 pm. I guided her into the living room to sit on the couch and then said it all at once.

"I love you, Mom, and I know you love me. I don't know how to tell you this and I don't want you to think that I am dying, but I have HIV."

She jolted, crossed her arm over her heart, and dropped her head in tears. This was the last news she wanted to hear.

"Do you know who you got it from?" she asked. I began to tell her about the things that had happened with Thomas and then Roam. She just held me, not saying a word for a moment. Then she kept telling me things would be all right, even with tears still flowing from her eyes. "Everything will be alright; just pray." I could tell I had hit my mom with news she didn't know how to process. I heard her in the middle of the night on her knees, praying and crying, crying and praying. I felt so bad. All I could do was think about the pain my mom was feeling. I wanted to run and hold her so bad, but she needed her moment. I just stayed in the next room listening to her hurt. There was nothing I could do about it. Who would want this life for their daughter? HIV is nothing fun. It's scary especially when you think about the old days. My mom was very old school. I couldn't imagine her thoughts.

The next morning, she asked me about my pills. I told her I would start my medication on the 7th. She encouraged me to take every pill they gave me. My mother was there for me and never loved me differently. Ever since I told my mother, I never had to fight a battle alone. She was so supportive and strong for me during my weak moments.

On September 7, my life changed forever. It was night one of my first pill. That Thursday night, I took my first antiviral pill. I decided to take my pills every night around 9:30 pm. I thought if I slept things off, I would dodge all the side effects that I had read about. At about 9 am, I started throwing up left and right. Every time I thought it was ending, more vomit and more vomit came. It was noon and I still was vomiting. I knew I was getting dehydrated because I couldn't eat, drink, or keep anything down. I slowly put on some easy-going clothes and to the emergency room I went. This was my first time going to the ER since my diagnosis, and so I had no idea what I was in for. Going to the hospital was by far the worst experience I had ever had. I was treated with so much disrespect. My doctor and nurse had no care in the world about my emotions. After revealing my status to the doctor, she informed the nurse. The nurse then told me to follow up with an HIV clinic instead of my primary health doctor. Her tone of voice was loud as she rolled her eyes, walking away. The only thing separating us from the other patients were curtains. I felt terrible after leaving that hospital. It was one of the worst mistakes I had ever made.

Later that day, I debated with myself about what time I should take my second pill. I believed that I took it too late the other night and my stomach probably did not have enough food. I didn't know what worked or didn't work. So, I decided to take my Zofran around 7 pm and my antiviral pill at 8:30 pm (September 8, pill 2). My second morning waking up since taking the antiviral pills, I was a little sick to the stomach. I took another Zofran around 9:00 am, because I had to be at work around 11 am and couldn't afford to start throwing up again.

Around 5 pm, I began to experience cramps in my right lower abdomen. At 6:42 pm, I couldn't walk. The pain was so bad.

"God, please take this pain away," I repeated over and over. I
didn't know if I was experiencing bad side effects or not. The
pain finally went away around 9 pm. At this point, I wasn't
about to take another pill. My stomach had been hurting
for hours and I had no idea why. I skipped my third pill on
September 9th. The next morning, I woke up (September 10)
and I felt normal. I decided to skip last night's dose. The
last two pills had me feeling bad. This was my only morning
waking up normal. I couldn't afford to be sick when I worked
until 11 pm that night. I would try to continue the medicine
that night around 8:30 pm. I was trying my best to allow
my body to get used to taking this pill. It was the weekend
and my doctor's office was closed. Around 4 pm, my girly
came on. Well, that explained the terrible stomach pain I
had experienced the day before. I was starting to get paranoid
about everything now. I had no idea that was the reason I was
in so much pain. My cycle was very irregular, so I couldn't
always pinpoint when it was coming. I guess that was good
news. At least I didn't vomit again. That day, I planned to eat
a snack around 5:30 pm, eat dinner at 7:30 pm, take a nausea
pill at 8 pm, and my medicine at 9 o'clock pm (pill 4). I prayed
for a good morning with zero side effects. September 11th
marked my fourth morning waking up since I started taking
antiviral medication. The night before, I took my pill around
9 o'clock. I made sure I had food in my stomach. I drank a
lot of fluid. It was 9 am the following morning and I had no
sick feeling. I prepared breakfast and took a nausea pill just in
case. I didn't feel like being sick and throwing up. Everything
seemed like it was starting to come together. So far, nausea
and vomiting my first morning of taking the pill seemed to

be my only side effect. At 10:30 pm, I just remembered to take my pill. I did eat a home-cooked meal and still felt full. Down it went, my fifth antiviral pill. Thank God I woke up on September 12th (fifth morning) with no sickness. I started to have some hope. I prayed that I continue my medicine with no sickness. That night, I took my medicine around 9:30 pm (pill 6). The following morning marked my sixth of seven pills on September 13th. I woke up to another morning of no sickness. I took my seventh pill. Because I skipped one of my pills, the next day would be the end of an official week for me. I prayed that I wouldn't get sick and that my body was finally adjusting to my medicine. September 14 was here, my seventh morning waking up after taking antiviral medicine. Yes, I finally survived my first week of taking antiviral pills with no more signs of side effects. It was hard. I even skipped a dose due to sickness. I kept on trying things, to find out what worked, until the only side effect I had was nausea. I just kept praying that my body would get used to the pills, so that I could take them without any sickness. Mentally, I had to keep telling myself that my body just had to get used to taking pills.

"I am going to get through this," I said over and over and over.

I managed to find a time to take my medicine that worked best for me. No matter what happened, I was not going back to the emergency room. I had been emotionally abused. I wasn't ashamed of my virus at the time, I had little to no thoughts at all, but that kind of treatment caught me off guard. Before going to the emergency room, I had been to the health department, the women's clinic, saw a therapist, an attorney, and told some friends about my HIV status. I was coping. No, I wasn't happy about my status, but I wasn't expecting that kind of judgment. Their entire body language said more than words could've ever spoken aloud. I got the message clear as day.

Two weeks later, I was waking up every day with no side effects. However, trying to get my body used to taking meds everyday was a huge challenge and it still is. My life took a lot of praying and a lot of self-determination. I almost gave up on taking pills because I was tired of feeling sick. After adjusting to my pills, I started thinking about Roam. I wanted him to know how much he had hurt me. During all the sickness I was experiencing, I didn't have time to focus on him. I thought I was dying inside. Things were so bad. I can't remember a time in my life when I had experienced such severe sickness like I did when taking antiviral medicine for the first time. Being alone through that process, I had no choice but to find self-motivation. I discovered strength inside me that I never knew was there. After three weeks of taking medicine, I decided to write Roam a letter. I just couldn't get over what Roam had done to me. I wanted him to know how much he had hurt me. My letter read:

Dear Roam,

I finally decided to stop contacting you. I will no longer call, text, or bother you in any way. I no longer have the strength inside me to continue to try to make things work. I no longer have the concern it takes to even care. You did something so bad to who knows how many women. Deep inside, I feel that you don't care, you feel no sorrow, and you think your excuses justify your actions. Nothing I ever did comes close to what you did to me. You may be sitting back laughing, but like my grandmother used to say, "Every dog will have its day." In a way, I thank you for redirecting my mindset. Without going through the impossible, I wouldn't know the possible. I looked up to you in ways I never did with no man. I trusted you. I cared for you. I never wanted to give up on us. It is kind of sad that I still feel you could've been the one for me. Love has no health status, no color, no age, and all you had to do was tell me the truth from the beginning. You were that perfect father in my eyes until you took advantage of someone else's daughter, someone else's sister. You took advantage of me. I don't wish any bad your way, because I am past that now. There was a time I was mad at the world; I was mad at everybody but myself. When I looked in the mirror and stopped blaming everybody else and reviewed myself, I found a way out; a way to a deeper happiness. I found all my hidden dark ways that I had to change. I found all my imperfections. I found my disobedience and ways that led me to the place of forgiveness. If you die today, don't worry about me. I am just fine. Even though I will never look the other way and because of you, I will forever have hurt in my heart. I can't take all the pain away today, tomorrow, next month, or next year, but someday, someday, and someday, I will."

After writing a letter to Roam, I fell deeper into my own thoughts. So much began to play a part in me pursuing charges against Roam. I started feeling partly responsible for not going to the doctor with him, not asking him for his checkup results or using a condom to protect myself during sex, and the other side of me feared stigma. I didn't want anyone to find out about my status. For God's sake, my first experience with HIV at the emergency room was unheard of. I was treated like people could've died touching me or talking to me. Taking Roam to court put everything I had going on the line. I knew what happened in court would be made available as public records. I could lose my business, my career, and no one would treat me the same. Would it all be worth it just for two years in jail? Two years! No one would remember Roam, but everyone would remember me. I was afraid, but I had to take that chance of losing all I had worked hard to build or walk away. A decision I never wanted to face. I wasn't ready for the world to know my status. I just wanted to breathe again; could I please breathe again? After being HIV positive myself, I see how hard it is. I understand doing things without thinking at all. After getting to know Roam before our falling out, I wondered if he could have been this big monster who gave me HIV on purpose. It was an answer I would never fully know. A part of me wanted to believe he didn't think he could give me the virus. If he was undetectable, he couldn't have given it to me. Did he get so depressed that he stopped taking his medicine? Something wasn't adding up to me and I had no way of knowing the full truth. HIV put me in a place I never thought I could be in. Was he wrong? Yes! It is not easy, especially when it feels like the world is against you. Should everyone run from you because you have cancer, diabetes, a skin disease, or anything that is not considered normal health? Do you wonder who also played a major part in my HIV status? I say, "STIGMA."

Now I had to continue to face mistreatment. I was already down about myself and didn't care to hear people assume how I contracted the virus. I couldn't continue like that. Stigma is like promoting suicide, depression, and low self-esteem. People better watch how they treat others. HIV can hit your home directly or indirectly. How will you feel if your daughter came home, sat you on the couch, and told you she was HIV POSITIVE? How fun would it be to hear this coming from your grandbabies?

These thoughts made me wonder if I really wanted Roam to go to prison for what he had done to me. Yes, I really did. At the same time, could stigma go to jail too? When asking myself that question, I became deadlocked with what decision to make. I didn't know if I should walk away, put him away, or both. His actions being intentional or unintentional was unclear. So, I dropped all charges against him. Some of my family and friends wished I would've done more. They felt he deserved to do time in prison. Who says he will not pay? Was I just as much to blame as Roam? If Thomas was positive, could he blame me one hundred percent? I had to take some part in what happened. Now I am not against someone pressing charges against the person who gave them HIV, if that state allows it. At times I wish I could go back on my decision to not pursue charges. For me, I don't think it was a win situation. It is just one of those individual decisions, but no one should be afraid to do what your heart is guiding you to do. I remember reading about ladies taking their mate to court. I had all respect for them, wishing I could've been there supporting them along the way. All I am saying is that the world makes it hard for people to reveal their status. No one knows the deep hurt I feel with HIV inside of me. After becoming more educated about HIV, I knew that I wasn't about to die. I could live a long productive life. I couldn't get totally mad at people for assuming things about HIV, even offering me a paper plate when I showed up to eat at certain people's homes. Prior to my diagnosis, I never took the time to research this virus in full detail. I was a part of the stigma to a degree, but never would I mistreat anyone. I probably would've thought someone with HIV was dying because of the old days. Mistreatment and judgment would never have been me.

CHAPTER 8

CAN I STILL LIVE?

I WAKE UP in the morning looking forward to eating and taking my daily medicine because I love me. I smile because I am still here. I still have moments to share with those who love me. I can still call my mom to say, I love you. I can still tell my sister she has a big head with that same gap in between her teeth since she was three years old, laughing. Well, I may have to duck and dodge just knowing she is going to throw something at my head to hit me, but I'm still her little sister. My life does not end here. I am still alive. I don't have anything standing in the way of me working and fulfilling my goals. Yes, I must take daily pills, visit my doctor every three to six months to ensure that I'm undetectable in order to protect my potential partner, exercise, and take vitamins to have more energy. No, I can't change the fact that I have HIV. Reality remains. I have my ups and downs mentally, still puzzled about the betrayal I feel inside. It's been a year since I was diagnosed with HIV. Boy, did I think my entire life was over? I thought I would never smile again, never go out with friends, never dress up, never feel good about myself, or anything that made me feel young and beautiful. I had no idea how to continue living. I thought no one would be interested in me. I thought no one would understand me. Even now, I hide my status from the public. I try to remain as private as I can. Maybe one day I will show my hand, expose my voice, and show my face. As I tell my story, some wonder if I am married. Did love ever find me? Am I happy? I am like I never was, at the most peaceful place with myself. I care about all of me. I must admit, I drew so much into loving myself that it is hard for me to open myself to someone else. I had been in such terrible relationships that I began to lose faith in me finding the man for me. After all, why would I want to get married? I was not about to settle for anything or anyone just because I was HIV positive. I learned my lesson early with Roam. I stopped hoping for a relationship. All I wanted was to find love within myself. I can remember when I first found out I was positive. I had very few people I could trust. I ran away from so many friends because I knew I couldn't trust them. There was only one friend who was so hard to get rid of: Richard. He and I were good friends; we went to school together. We planned several dates in the past, but something always seemed to come up which caused us to cancel every time. I know all chances of us dating now are over. As he continued to inbox me like he has always done, I knew I had to tell him my darkest secret. I just didn't want to lead him on and get his hopes up for a future with me. I prayed that he was someone I could trust and just move on from there. How could I reveal such news like this? This would come out of the blue to him. How would he react and who would he tell? We know the same people for God's sake, I remember thinking. So, I decided to tell him half the truth but enough to give him the facts. I told him that my ex cheated on me and received a positive HIV test while I was still undergoing testing myself. I told him that there was a good chance that mine would be positive. I also said that my doctor declared me to be undetectable to the point that I could no longer pass the virus to anyone else, but I still would have the virus forever. He got so quiet on the phone. I could tell he was not expecting any of that.

"When will you know?" he eventually asked. "I won't stop talking to you and your secrets stay with me."

I just knew he wanted to stay on a friend's level for good now. The next day, I remember him texting me about Magic Johnson and his wife. I just knew he was encouraging me to keep my head up. The third day, he asked if I could sleep with him. "Why would I sleep with you, I don't want to have sex with anyone?" I angrily asked. "No, I meant stay on the phone and fall asleep together, silly girl." "Thanks for the clarity, my bad." Then I told him, "You know there's a very good chance that I will have HIV." He told me that my results would come back fine. I replied, "No, my chances are very high, and my doctor told me that it's not showing in my blood yet."

I was so uncomfortable just telling him I was HIV positive. I did and said everything to get him to realize how serious my situation was. A week later, he asked me if I was considered HIV positive and what did the doctor mean about me having the virus and the virus not being in my blood yet. At that point, I knew I had to have this conversation with him. I thought he had gotten the big picture, but it was clear he hadn't. I was upset. Did I not tell him that I would have the virus forever? What questions did he still have? Why force answers out of me when we didn't have any chance of being together? So, I began to push away. I avoided answering his question. He would call me and every time I rushed off the phone with him. I told him that I was just finding myself and I didn't want to be stressed. He wouldn't give up. One day he called, and I remember yelling out loud on the phone with him, "I am positive, just forget everything I told you before and know that I am HIV positive. Are you happy now?" I asked him. I couldn't believe those words came out of my mouth. It was my first time ever saying those words aloud. I just wanted him to leave me alone. I wasn't fixable to have a future with. I explained my results to him. My doctor told me that I was undetected, meaning that there was not enough of the virus to detect in my blood. I told him that there was effectively no risk of HIV transmission during sex with a person determined to have an undetectable viral load, but I still was positive for the virus (HIV Treatment as Prevention, 2020).

He replied, "I won't leave you because of the virus, I want you, the person inside of you." I thought for sure he was just being nice. I knew him from years prior to this virus thing. I knew deep down that we had likings for each other a long time now and he didn't want to be mean to me.

We continued being friends and three months later he asked that we become official. This just couldn't be real. Was he serious? I kept telling myself it was all a joke. I needed time to really think about it. So many emotions were running through my head. What did this man want from me? Why wasn't he running for his life? Why waste time on me? Why, tell me?

Despite my questions, we went back to talking all day, every day. We began to make a habit of falling asleep on the phone every night. He called me every lunch break even if it was just for five minutes. He made sure he was present in my life, highly consistent. Soon enough, my heart began to smile again, but I felt afraid. I was starting to care for another man, who accepted me when he didn't have to. He provided his shoulder for me to cry on, and spent hours talking to me. Now I found myself waking up in the middle of the night when he is not on the phone with me. I was attached to hearing him breathe. In the back of my mind, I didn't believe he would stay with me after he realized how serious the situation was. I believed he would soon leave, so I told myself I couldn't fall too deep. I had to find a way out of the way I was feeling. Loving all over again was not something I was ready for.

Despite my frustration, I agreed to go on a date. After all this time we were talking on the phone, I could at least spend time with him in person. He was my friend if nothing else. So, I met him at a BBQ place. I ordered ribs, mac & cheese, and baked beans. He had a pork sandwich and fries. I had to have been very hungry or the food was just so good that it caused me to lick the sauce off my fingers. During the dinner, I remember smiling and laughing while looking into his eyes. It awakened my emotions; I was in love. Out of all the talks we had, not one of our conversations was about my body directly. He never was inappropriate with me. He only asked for my time, my talks, and to sleep with me. On the phone was all the sleeping he wanted, to hear me snoring, to hear my body movements as I tossed and turned at night. He grew to become my peace. I could sleep better. I no longer woke up in the middle of the night. I built a love for him that I would never lose.

Two months after bonding, he made an epic decision. Seeing him on one knee felt like a daydream.

"Will you marry me, Hope, will you marry me? You are rib from my rib, my piece of heaven. I will not go another day without you as my wife. I will not go another hour without you in my life," Richard said.

I had no idea this day was coming. Less than three months of dating and here I was, faced with making an important decision.

"NO," I answered. I couldn't marry a man that was HIV negative. He could never understand my pain, never understand me, and would use my status against me someday, I thought. He was so heartbroken. He asked me to give him space and began to walk away.

"Wait," I called out to him.

"Wait, wait for what?" he asked. "I love you, but I love you enough to give you more time too. I have watched you rebuild yourself up when suicide was knocking at your door. I felt your anxiety, your depression even when I was away from you. I will not rest until I add happiness inside your heart. Even though you are still standing, I know you are still broken. I will not hurt you, just marry me."

I was confused to the highest degree. Oh, my God! I hadn't made myself available to anyone since Roam. I just yelled, "No," again and again, "Noooo." Then Richard left. Days after turning Richard down, I got a call from Thomas. He asked if he could come by to talk. I said "Yes." I hadn't spoken to Thomas in months. He showed up and we discussed his results (although he never showed his paperwork, after being asked). He said he was negative and talked about how everything went down and how he regretted the way he did things. He felt like he should've been more patient, supportive, and understanding.

"I forgive you, Thomas," I said and went on saying, "If you never would've been out cheating on me, this never would've happened. All I wanted was for you to love only me. Thomas,

I never imagined myself with somebody else. I didn't know that was possible."

I was blaming him instead of myself. Just because he did what he did, didn't make him responsible. I had a choice to leave him sooner even if I had to go back to my parents. I also had a choice to woman up and take care of myself. I had a choice to use protection when having sex with the new guy. I couldn't continue to fault Thomas for what Roam did to me, but I did fault him for not being a friend. I began to cry all over again. Thomas looked at me and said, "Hope, I know you are a good woman. I remember all the things you did for me. I know how you supported and pushed me in my career. You stayed for years while I played games and to be honest, I can't find another woman like you. The bond we had is stronger than HIV. Even though I don't have it, will you be with me?"

As he dropped to his knees with a ring in his hand, I said a big no before he could even pop the question.

"Thomas, I came to you first with the news. Even though I thought you gave me HIV, I still wanted to choose you. I wanted to face it with you. Never would I have thought you would've turned your back on me. When I was down facing suicide to the point of wanting to jump off a roof, I had no way to call out for you. I needed you. I cannot and will not marry you." I asked him to leave my home. He did after kissing me on the forehead.

I called Richard immediately and I was crying. I told him what happened. Like always, he was there for me.

I started to read the Bible and understand the relationship between Adam and Eve. It made me regret saying "No" to Richard. I didn't tell him that, but I did tell him that I was feeling happier since he showed up. I asked him to go to church with me and he did. Two months after spending even more time together, Richard proposed to me again.

"Will you marry me, Hope?" This time he was proposing on the phone because his job had him hours away from me.

"Yes, Richard, I will marry you. I am in love with you and I pray you don't break my heart. I cannot afford another heartbreak. If you going to play games with me, please let me be, if you're not, then I accept marrying you," I told him.

He was so happy. He called his mother and told her he was going to marry me. Then he asked my family for permission. What a dream come true. I was getting married.

Sadly, for me, I wasn't as happy as I thought I would be. I was too damaged to be excited inside like any woman would want to be. This was a dream come true. When he got back from his job, he had gotten me a ring and again he proposed. I was excited and I agreed yet again. Although we wanted to be married as soon as possible, we both realized how our parents would kill us if we didn't give them the opportunity to support us, so we didn't rush to the courthouse.

I would be marrying my long-term best friend. This man accepts all of me. When I want to give up on fighting, he reminds me that he is right beside me, fighting with me. I must say that all my bad days worked together for good. It took me separating myself to focus more on my faith. I am one thankful person today. I won't take anymore side cuts. I trust my Father and I make it my obligation to follow my Father.

Later, I would get to hear that Thomas and his baby's mother broke up for good. He felt off and even attempted suicide himself. She put him on child support and continued seeing other men. I pray for him daily that his life will be filled with merciful blessings. The only thing I will always not have an answer to is "Why he wasn't there for me?" I guess I will never know. As I start my new journey, I know there will be upcoming challenges to face. That is just life within itself. If somebody were to ask me my worst fear, I would say it is transmitting the virus to my husband someday. Even though I've remained at an undetectable stage since I was diagnosed, I still fear the unknown. Like, what happens if I skip my pills? What about our future kids? Even though HIV is changing, even a 1% chance of passing it to my family is 1% too much to think about. I couldn't live with myself if I gave my own child HIV. Will I even be able to have kids after all my health issues? I try to conquer this fear by deepening my knowledge about STDs/HIV as much as possible. I also think about the longevity of my future marriage. It is obvious that I am still a work in progress and all my obstacles are clearly not over yet.

I give up! I give up trying to fight a battle that is not mine to fight; a battle that is already won. No matter what happens, I know it is somehow God's plan. In the end, I will be just fine. I stand here as a woman of no regrets. My life is mine and I claim every moment of it. One thing that I've learned is that I can't allow anyone else to fill the happiness in my heart. I have to own my own joy. I can't even depend on Richard or any other man to give me the strength I need to carry on with my day. Nobody but God gave me life, so no one can stop me from living it.

The next day I got up and told my fiancée to take me to church. I told him God had spoken and I was ready now. I am ready to share my testimony. We pulled up to the church just in time for me to walk up to the altar. My fiancée stood right there behind me. I asked the pastor for permission to share my testimony. "If the Lord guided you here, we need to hear what you got to say," he said while handing me the microphone with honor. With all eyes on me, I began to speak without fear.

"As I stand before you today, I stand before you perfectly imperfect. I stand before you by the mercy of God speaking from my own personal experiences. I been through some things that many will never admit to. Imagine going to the doctor hearing that you're HIV POSITIVE…Can you imagine being on the edge of a roof ready to commit suicide? I wanted to end my life, but today I stand here being thankful of the woman I'm becoming, the woman God created me to be. I came here today with a message to the younger generation. Don't go around living life thinking that tomorrow you can make things right. Tomorrow may never come. Stop giving your body to every man you date because he's cute or driving a nice car and flattering you with gifts that you never had before. Don't be fooled by his lust or material things. Your standards shall be much more than that. The same way God brings blessings, all the gifts in the world, the devil can put on a bow tie to cover up his empty box. Don't be fooled. And just because you used to do this, and you used to do that doesn't mean that God has given up on you. Don't listen to those that judge you and make you feel like it's too late to turn around. You are worth saving. You're worth prioritizing. You're worth patience. You're worth changing for. This is an evil world and it's time to protect you. I've been on the right side and the wrong side. I've been betrayed and I have gone out for revenge. I grew bitter. I was hurt and I hurt. But today, God said let it go. Healing time is now. Respecting your body starts now. I thank Jesus for saving me. As I walk this perfect imperfect life, I look forward to sharing more of my story. In closing, I would like for you all to know that it is true, Jesus saves."

As I put down the mic, people started clapping, the room was louder than I ever heard before. Ladies started walking up to me with all the hugs and kisses they could give, while the men passed out handshakes. I began making my way to the exit door after revealing everything I had to say, and Richard proceeded behind me. I cried tears of joy. The choir begin to sing a song, "Jesus, you are everything I need and Jesus… you are everything I dreamed. Jesus, you are everything I need and Jesus…you are everything that I've dreamed." On my way back home, I felt closure. When I got home, the song from church just was stuck in my head. "Jesus, you are everything I need and Jesus…you are everything that I've dreamed," I mumbled while preparing for bed. I just knew that Jesus saved me.

THE END

Silently Betrayed Vol. 1

Quotes by
Latosha Faulkner

"Together we are powerful, individually we lack something."

"Everyone should reach a certain level of self-capacity before adding anyone to their life."

"Stop giving first-class seats to people who're offering you the last seat on the bus."

"Dreams become more than dreams once actions are put in place to accomplish them."

"No one can see your vision so no one can correctly lead your vision."

"To accomplish a plan toward success, you must follow and study those who have already succeeded."

"My power is not in the hands of the next person, but in the spirit of God."

"If healing takes time, why spend your time unhealed?"

*"Waiting on a familiar face to support you
will leave you waiting forever."*

*"You cannot change the truth because you
don't like the tongue that spoke it."*

"The key to failure is wishing it on someone else."

"No one can stop a smile you choose to have."

*"Just because the bullet didn't hit you, doesn't mean
you forget how close you were to that bullet."*

*"Sometimes you have to forgive the unforgivable
in order to break through the unbreakable."*

"Never mistreat someone who deserves to be rewarded."

TIPS: TRY NOT TO BECOME A VICTIM TO HIV

1. *ASK, are you HIV positive?*

2. *Prior to having sex, request medical records off the TOP.*

3. *SEE THE RESULTS WITH YOUR OWN EYES.*

4. *Go to the health department with your partner and review their results (the HD will print them a copy once they submit their ID).*

5. *ASK THEM: When was your last HIV test? (I would only accept results within the last three months.) A person could've slept with someone new last night and it may take 3-6 months to show that they're HIV positive.*

6. *USE CONDOMS especially when you only have that person's word (condoms do protect you against HIV).*

7. *If you're having unprotected sex with someone who's HIV positive, make sure their viral loads are*

undetectable (according to the CDC, a person with undetectable status cannot pass HIV to their partner).

8. *Go to the doctor/clinic with your partner to provide support.*

TIPS-TRY NOT TO BECOME A VICTIM TO HIV

1. *Don't have more than one sex partner.*

2. *Don't cheat because your current partner is cheating... Know that it's okay to be by yourself until the right person comes along.*

3. *Don't have unprotected sex.*

4. *Get an HIV test 1-2 times per year.*

5. *Don't go on their word alone with no proof of results.*

6. *Be aware of the prescriptions your partner is taking and get information from a pharmacy or research if you are unsure about what the prescription is used to treat.*

7. *If you suspect something strange, Google the pill (some people change bottles to hide the truth).*

8. *Pay attention to the person's daily routine (a person can be taking pills daily and you ignored it).*

9. *Get EDUCATED and stop the stigma against HIV.*

10. *If a person reveals their status to you, keep it to yourself so that they feel comfortable being honest with the next person. You can politely tell them no if you're not comfortable moving forward with them, but assure them that you will keep their health information confidential. This will help them continue to be honest with other people.*

Q&A by the Author

1) Do you have to be gay to get HIV?

   No, you do not have to be gay to have HIV.

   However, having anal sex involves a higher risk of infection.

   - Truvada is a medication that can help prevent HIV (ask your doctor about this pill to see if it's necessary).

2) How do I get more accurate information about HIV?

   CDC.com and review the bibliography at the end of this book.

3) How do I get help paying for treatment?

   Visit the health department in your state for assistance.

4) What kind of doctor should I go see?

   The health department in your state can help you

find a doctor and set up treatments. Infectious disease specialists can treat clients with HIV.

5) Where can I get an affordable HIV test?

Health department in your state or ask your primary care doctor.

6) Should I reveal my HIV status to the world?

Revealing your status is not necessary if you are not sexually involved with that person. Check the laws in your state because some states don't require a person to share their status if they are undetectable for six months when having protected sex. I personally would want the person I'm having sex with to know everything about me.

7) Should I tell anyone at all?

You can tell people you trust if you need additional support (someone to talk to).

- When having sex with someone, you should always use protection unless it is an agreement between both parties (check the laws regarding HIV in your state as they are constantly changing).

- I recommend asking yourself, "If a person doesn't accept you for you, are they worth being around?"

8) What medication should I take?

Talk with your healthcare provider, everybody's situation is different. If you have a hard time swallowing big pills, ask your doctor about smaller pill options.

9) Can I still date and have a sexual relationship?

Yes, love is bigger than HIV.

There are people in relationships where one partner is negative and the other one is positive or both partners are positive.

- Never think HIV will stop you from being in a relationship.

- Talk to your healthcare provider about the chances of passing HIV and things you or your partner can do to protect themselves.

- It is known that a person is not able to spread HIV after becoming undetectable.

10) Can I still have kids?

Yes, get approval from your doctor and allow your doctor to set up a plan for you to have kids. Everybody's situation is different and it's best to talk to your doctor regarding the chances of passing HIV to your child before deciding.

11) Is my life over?

No, people are living long productive lives with HIV.

Your chances of surviving can depend on several things, talk to your healthcare provider. There are people who have been living with HIV/AIDS for 20-30 years and still counting.

12) Should you press charges on your partner?

Your personal decision!

It is not wrong to press charges because no one has the right to expose someone while hiding their status and not knowing for sure if they're undetectable.

13) Is suicide the answer?

No, it never is!

Please call the National Suicide Prevention Lifeline

@ 1-800-273-8255

Someone is there to listen to your problems, support you, and share resources to help put you in the right direction.

MESSAGE FROM
THE AUTHOR

We all have been in a situation that could've gone totally differently from how it went. I tell people all the time, *"Just because the bullet didn't hit you, doesn't mean you forget how close you were to that bullet."* When you go through stuff in life and make it out without facing lifetime consequences, be thankful. Don't go about life belittling or judging those who weren't so lucky. At the end of the day, we all have somethings in life we must deal with. You can be up today and down tomorrow. You can easily be in the next person's shoes. Life is not promising anything to anyone. I encourage everyone to take life for what it is today and live your life the best way you know how. In the process of it all, take care of yourself.

When it comes to your health, don't expect anyone to care about your health more than you. I encourage every one of my readers to get an STD/HIV test, Pap smear, and required checkups on time. Whether you're suffering from high blood pressure, sickle cells, diabetes, HIV, AIDs, a UTI, grieving the loss of a loved one, or your life is just plain out perfect, take care of you. You can't take care of a situation you don't know about. Don't be afraid to find out the results you need to live longer; like with anything, if left untreated it gets worse. Let's take steps to living as long as we can. And remember, *"No one can stop a smile you choose to have."*

Contact the Author

(Allow up to 1-7 business days to respond)
Facebook: https://m.facebook.com/Defeatdapurposefirst
Email: defeatdapurpose@gmail.com
Website: www.defeatdapurpose.com

Support DefeatdaPurpose, LLC! Let us put an end to the spread of HIV. I plan to offer a listening ear to as many individuals as possible who need someone to talk to. Help me dedicate as much of my time as possible to making a difference in someone's life that could be your son or daughter. I am not just supporting women but also men. I have no judgement at all. You will defeat the purpose formed to destroy you.

CashApp: $Youcanlive
PayPal: defeatdapurpose@gmail.com

For more information about DefeatdaPurpose, LLC go to www.defeatdapurpose.com

For more accurate information about HIV, go to www.cdc.com.

Bibliography

Fact Sheets | Resource Library | HIV/AIDS | CDC. Retrieved from https://www.cdc.gov/hiv/library/factsheets/index.html

Global Statistics | HIV.gov. Retrieved from https://www.hiv.gov/hiv-basics/overview/data-and-trends/global-statistics

HIV Basics | HIV.gov. Retrieved from https://www.hiv.gov/hiv-basics

HIV Basics | HIV/AIDS | CDC. Retrieved from https://www.cdc.gov/hiv/basics/index.html

HIV/AIDS Facts, Symptoms, Treatment & Prevention. Retrieved from https://www.emedicinehealth.com/hivaids/article_em.htm

HIV/AIDS: The Basics | Understanding HIV/AIDS | AIDS info. Retrieved from https://aidsinfo.nih.gov/understanding-hiv-aids/fact-sheets/19/45/hiv-aids--the-basics

HIV Treatment as Prevention. (2020, March 03). Retrieved June 1, 2020 from https://www.cdc.gov/hiv/risk/art/index.html

How Has Magic Johnson Survived 20 Years with HIV? Retrieved from https://www.livescience.com/16909-magic-johnson-hiv-aids-anniversary.html

National Suicide Prevention Lifeline. Retrieved from https:// suicidepreventionlifeline.org/

Suicide Prevention | Youth.gov. Retrieved from https://youth. gov/youth-topics/youth-suicide-prevention

Suicide Violence Prevention Injury Center CDC. Retrieved from https://www.cdc.gov/violenceprevention/ suicide/index.html

What Is HIV / AIDS & How Do You Get It? Retrieved from https://www.plannedparenthood.org/learn/ stds-hiv-safer-sex/hiv-aids